'What a beautiful thing this little book is, packed with honest accounts of what people do to make themselves feel better.'

– from the Foreword by Cathy Rentzenbrink, author of
The Last Act of Love *and* A Manual for Heartache

★ ★ ★ ★ ★

'A love letter to hobbies, this book is full of powerful stories of joy-sparking activities that cut through the fug, lift us up and make each day a little brighter. It's a manifesto for learning and laughing that gives us permission to exercise a brilliant form of self-care.'

– Pooky Knightsmith, internationally renowned
child and adolescent mental health expert

★ ★ ★ ★ ★

'This is a great big hug of a book. It's like chatting to an old friend who's wise, funny and says exactly what you need to hear.'

– Dave Chawner, award-winning comic, presenter and mental
health campaigner and author of Weight Expectations

WHAT I DO TO GET THROUGH

by the same author

The Recovery Letters
Addressed to People Experiencing Depression
Edited by James Withey and Olivia Sagan
Afterword by Tom Couser
ISBN 978 1 78592 183 4
eISBN 978 1 78450 460 1

related titles

We're All Mad Here
The No-Nonsense Guide to Living with Social Anxiety
Claire Eastham
Afterword by Natasha Devon MBE
ISBN 978 1 78592 082 0
eISBN 978 1 78450 343 7

Unlock Your Resilience
Strategies for Dealing with Life's Challenges
Stephanie Azri
Foreword by Rachel Kelly
ISBN 978 1 78775 102 6
eISBN 978 1 78775 103 3

Hell Yeah Self-Care!
A Trauma-Informed Workbook
Alex Iantaffi and Meg-John Barker
ISBN 978 1 78775 245 0
eISBN 978 1 78775 246 7

What I Do to Get Through

How to Run, Swim, Cycle, Sew, or Sing Your Way Through Depression

Edited by
Olivia Sagan and James Withey

Illustrated by Sophie Standing
Foreword by Cathy Rentzenbrink

Jessica Kingsley Publishers
London and Philadelphia

First published in Great Britain in 2021 by Jessica Kingsley Publishers
An Hachette Company

I

Copyright © Olivia Sagan and James Withey 2021
Illustrations copyright © Sophie Standing 2021
Foreword copyright © Cathy Rentzenbrink 2021

Trigger Warning: This book mentions anxiety, depression and suicide.

A CIP catalogue record for this title is available from the British Library
and the Library of Congress

ISBN 978 1 78775 298 6
eISBN 978 1 78775 299 3

Printed and bound in Great Britain by Clays Ltd

Jessica Kingsley Publishers' policy is to use papers that are natural,
renewable and recyclable products and made from wood grown in
sustainable forests. The logging and manufacturing processes are expected
to conform to the environmental regulations of the country of origin.

Jessica Kingsley Publishers
Carmelite House
50 Victoria Embankment
London EC4Y 0DZ

www.jkp.com

For my father, who couldn't float in the waves
Olivia

For Anya, Caitlin, Peter, Isabel, Olivia and Martha
James

CONTENTS

FOREWORD

Cathy Rentzenbrink

What a beautiful thing this little book is, packed with honest accounts of what people do to make themselves feel better. Not better as in 'fixed', you understand, but better as in just a bit better able to cope with life's ups and downs.

I have been in and out of depression since I was 19. I used to view it as a howling beast over which I had no control. It would arrive unbidden in the night and strip me of everything. There were times I feared I wouldn't survive. Over the last few years, with the help of some very good therapy, I try to see it more like the weather. Sometimes the clouds gather, sometimes the rain can feel a bit relentless, but there are things I can do. I'm not powerless. When I'm well, I can think everything through and set up some strategies for when my mood darkens. I can get a good raincoat and keep my wellies by the front door. I can learn how to sit out the storm and not do anything to make it all worse. I can try to not get stuck in despair but to move along an emotional range. I don't aim as high as happiness or contentment; it might seem violently impossible that I could ever be happy again, and dwelling on this only distresses me. But if I lower my expectations of both life and myself, that is a good start, and then I try to cultivate curiosity. If I can feel curious, then I can get some momentum going. If I can feel curious, then hope no longer feels so far away. And once I get to hope, the world brightens up again.

Reading has always been my number-one ally, but in recent years I have developed a wider toolbox of things that make me feel better, and, as for many of the contributors here, that includes being outside, walking, running, yoga, singing and meditation. The most important thing is that I am easy and gentle, and that I resist the temptation to turn any new hobby into a stick with which to beat myself. We are all different, of course, but I have never met a person prone to depression who doesn't have this tendency to self-flagellation. We could all do to turn up the volume on our self-compassion, to be kind to ourselves and find ways of making ourselves feel better that don't ultimately make us feel worse. I no longer drink alcohol because it turbo-charged my depression and I have learned to love the simple pleasure of sober life.

To stay sane, I have to maintain a faith in humanity. This can be hard to do when consuming news or looking at my phone, but much easier if I get out into the real world. I try to give people the benefit of the doubt and I look for the kindness of strangers. And that's what this book is. Some kind strangers offering the things they do that help. Take from it what you will; be kind and easy and gentle with yourself. One of the things I learned to do is a Buddhist mediation called Loving Kindness. It encourages me to wish good things for myself, and for everyone else, whether or not I know or like them. So that is what I wish for you, dear reader. From any pen to your heart, I wish you well as you continue on your journey through this cruel and beautiful life.

Cathy Rentzenbrink is the author of *A Manual for Heartache*.

INTRODUCTION

James Withey

It's always been my firm view that cuddling baby pandas should be on prescription.

In fact, so should annual three-month holidays to Antigua, free chocolate fountains and weekly play sessions with exuberant six-week-old Labrador puppies.

After the success of *The Recovery Letters*, we wanted to write a follow-up that would continue to help all of us on this wavy, strange, dizzying path of recovery. We wanted to hear more stories from people like you and me, who live alongside depression and other mental illnesses.

We kept hearing how people had found things in their life that make them feel better. Things that make their illness more bearable, that gave them meaning, relief, hope and – dare we say the word – some happiness. 'I wouldn't be alive without climbing,' we kept hearing or, 'It might sound odd, but I can honestly say knitting has helped me more than anything else.' The more we heard, the less odd it seemed. In fact, it made total sense.

With the long wait for talking therapies and the mixed results of antidepressants, we have to find things that work alongside (or instead of) the medical options. When mental illness strikes, we need tools at our side – and I'm not talking a large monkey wrench here. We have to find activities in our life that distract, heal, exorcise and calm.

Like the last book, you don't need to read this one from start to finish – we know how hard that can be. Pick it up, flick through it and find something that catches your eye. And remember, there might be times when some of the stories trigger thoughts that are distressing, so go gently.

You won't necessarily like the sound of each hobby, but read these stories with an open mind and don't be like me and dismiss activities that might work. 'Oh no, that's not for me.' I've said that too often, to too many things, then when I've tried them, I've found a lot of them work.

For example, I was never really one for exercise. Why sweat profusely in front of total strangers, gasping for your last breath and looking like an unconscious crow that's been dragged out of a stagnant canal? But once I started going to the gym, I found it helped. Admittedly,

I still don't know what most of the machines actually do – they all look like Italian sausage makers to me. And my rules are pretty simple: don't compare yourself with the muscly people on the ground floor in the tight red shorts. Don't compare yourself with the lithe, toned gods and goddesses on the second floor who don't seem to sweat at all. Get some really, really cheesy music on your phone and, most importantly, wear your worst possible outfit because, A, you're going to look like crap after ten minutes anyway, so what's the point? And, B, it balances out all the other people in ludicrously expensive, multi-functional, lycra-hugging, sculpted designer gym wear.

Now, we're definitely, definitely (definitely) not saying, 'Just do some extreme paragliding, it will completely cure your mental illness!' There's quite enough of those kind of ridiculous claims on the internet already. But we are saying, 'Do you know what? It might well help, and, damn it, we need all the help we can get.' If decoupaging an old chest of drawers with purple Peruvian kitten wallpaper makes a difference, then don't judge it – just do it. If you find kayaking with your chinchilla alleviates some of the pain, then hurrah, let's get out on the water more often.

If you try something and it doesn't work for you, give something else a go and don't add it to the mental list of things you can't do, because, hey, that's seems long enough anyway, right?

Just try to say, 'That didn't work for me; I'll try some crocheting/fishing/running/knitting/pottery/hillwalking/origami/yoga/dogwalking/boxing/photography/meditation/horse riding/cycling/decoupaging...instead.'

SEA SWIMMING

Virginia Jones

Picture this: A cold crisp winter's day on the beach, wind whipping along the shore, foreboding pewter-coloured waves and...a bunch of scantily clad people smiling and squealing in the sea. I'm likely to be one of them. I swim in the sea, all year round, to keep my anxiety and depression at bay.

When I first looked to understand how this works for me, I had to consider how my mental health moods manifest themselves. Everyone with a mental health diagnosis or struggling to manage their wellbeing experiences very unique moods, feelings or thoughts, although there are themes that resonate with many sufferers. Here are some of my most common ones.

Most of the time I see the world in black and white, devoid of colour, devoid of joy. The flip side to this is that when I occasionally experience joy, it is so completely, indescribably wonderful – it's like the moment when Dorothy lands in Oz and suddenly there is colour.

I can be happy and content, but unadulterated joy is very rare and only happens when I'm completely present and in the moment. When it happens, I find myself scrabbling around for ways to recreate it, which, as you can imagine, is counterproductive and pushes me into the waiting arms of the 'mental monkeys'.

The 'mental monkeys' is the name I have given to the constant internal dialogue in my brain. They don't miss a trick and are very rarely quiet. Any opportunity to chatter about situations out of my control, inconsequential self-enforced deadlines missed, what people think about me, did I say or do the right thing. You get the idea. They have no concept of night or day and will happily fill my brain with their negative opinions and questions 24/7. When I am tired or overwhelmed and my resilience threshold is low, there is a veritable chimps' tea party going on in there, one which I am not enjoying!

Being overwhelmed is my normal state *du jour*. At times,

self-inflicted, as I chase the elusive joy by filling my life with lots of things to do. Accepting every invitation to prove I can be 'normal'. Self-destruction button well and truly engaged. If I don't get the rest and respite I need, I'm liable to shut down. This doesn't happen quietly like a worn-out battery; it will be accompanied by a lot of angry noise before I lock myself away for varying lengths of time depending on how tired I am. Just acting like a 'normal' person can leave me shattered by around teatime.

This list is not exhaustive, but just indicative of how I feel most of the time. So what does sea swimming do for me to keep anxiety and depression at bay?

Sea swimming, as a pastime, is joyful. Instead of constantly trying to orchestrate feelings of pleasure and elation, the sea provides it. I swim with a great bunch of people a few times a week and we play in the water. Literally play like children. We connect as community and we laugh hard and long. Even on the bleakest of days, I never regret a swim, and there is always a warm welcome. The post-swim high can last for hours after the event, and knowing that the sea is a constant and therefore I have a constant supply of joy, it buoys me up.

When I'm in the sea, the endless negative internal dialogue is silenced. The sea overloads all of my senses, silky water on my skin, salty tastes and smells, shingle sounds, blue sights. The sound of the mental monkeys is quite literally drowned out.

The repetitive activity of stroke after stroke gives me space to collect my thoughts. I used to shy away from mindfulness exercises and meditation, too afraid it would give the mental monkeys free rein. What I have discovered is that the exact opposite happens – I have my best thoughts and ideas in the sea. The cluttered brain fog clears with the sea breeze.

The rest and respite I need, so that I don't feel over-whelmed, is easily achieved at the beach. You can't take your phone into the sea and you can't hear it beeping on the beach when you're in the water. The constant scrolling images and high-pitched sounds are replaced by a never-changing horizon.

I swim year round, in freezing temperatures and chal-lenging sea states. Putting myself in these situations on a regular basis, I'm exposing my body and mind to stress. Getting into wavy cold water is stressful for your body and mind, but I cope. I have adapted to deal with this stress, and it helps me go on to deal with everyday stress. When I'm swimming in these conditions, I can only be concerned about myself, in that moment, in that situation – there is no room to be concerned with anything else.

Other people think you are mad for swimming in the sea, all year round, and I own that label! Being in the sea reminds me that my depression and anxiety is transient; it ebbs and flows like the tide. It provides me with the opportunity to check in with myself, to see if another episode is on the horizon.

If you want to give wild swimming a go, search on the internet to find a group near you; there has been a huge increase in the popularity of wild swimming. We live in strange times, which humans were not designed for. Many of us have found ways to escape, to be our unaffected selves for just a moment, recapturing those feelings of possibility.

Although dark times are part of my illness, sea swimming provides a break in the clouds. I didn't choose to feel this way, but I've chosen how I deal with it on a day-to-day basis.

I have found a safe haven when my seas are stormy.

YOGA

Kelly Jensen

The first time I found the courage to attend a yoga class, I shook from the minute I walked in the door until the final minutes. In the gentlest of poses, my heart rattled against my chest, and my breath, unlike the rhythmic sounds of those around me, caught in my lungs and my throat.

Despite the overwhelming anxiety I felt being in that space and trying something new for myself, I felt good, even empowered, when I headed home. I took that first step. My brain fought against it and repeatedly told me lies about how terrible I was and how dumb I looked. But I was able to acknowledge those messages for what they were – and then let them go. *That* was why I shook.

Letting go is work.

After a few more yoga sessions, I learned how to shake less. How to walk to my mat without fearing I might pass out. How to let myself breathe. When I could do those things, I was also able to hear the wisdom my teacher shared: Every day is different. Everybody needs something different, which means it's important to honor what it is you need right here and right now. Yoga isn't about how far you could go or how much you can push yourself. It's not about what your neighbor is doing or what they look like. It's about finding comfort in the poses and being able to breathe with ease.

With that insight, suddenly everything about my own mental health made sense. For so long, I believed the answer to feeling better was in pushing to do things that were good for me or that would allow me to ignore my mind. To ignore pain or the feelings of discomfort I found, to ignore the insecurity and the myriad of ways I felt like an impostor in my own life. We're taught culturally that engaging in activities to forget about our feelings is healing. That it's being strong.

But mental health is not a light switch you turn on and off. It's a dial you, and only you, learn how to manage. Yoga, despite some of the popular media manifestations, is not about rigidity. It's not about grace or making pretty shapes. It's about being flexible, about finding balance between strength and ease, about honoring your own body, mind, and breath. Yoga is the practice of being non-competitive: you don't try to do what the person next to you is doing because you are not that person and you don't necessarily need what they need.

Moreover, you can't compete with yourself. You'll always be as strong as you were the week before, but your body might be asking you to not push to that limit this week. It may want you to turn your attention to breathing. That, sometimes, is the hardest work.

Yoga is also about learning to stumble, to fall, and to pick yourself back up again and listen to your body tell you whether today's the day you try again or the day you acknowledge that what you really need is the time to rest. No one but you can make those choices. It's called a practice, not a routine, for good reason.

Just like my regular yoga practice is about finding comfort and honoring my body, every day that I wake up is another day of finding comfort on the dial that is mental health. Some days I run colder. Other days, hotter. But in observing those shifts along the dial, I'm able to serve myself with what I need right where I am. I meet myself and I greet myself where I am. I don't push too hard when I can't, and I let myself expand and grow where I can.

I'm learning, day by day, to practice loving myself right where I am.

BIRDWATCHING

Paul Brook

I know that everything around you feels grey at the moment. I know you feel dragged down, burdened by the anxiety that chews away at your stomach, and the depression that pounds your brain. I know that your mind won't stop whirring. I know you don't look forward to anything anymore, and that it's hard to imagine finding anything exciting ever again.

But I also know that there's something that can help – birds. Yes, birds.

I'm going to describe a scene for you.

You're on the edge of a heath, in a strip of woodland. You're walking along a wide dirt path, with silver birches and bogs on either side. A great spotted woodpecker has just whizzed across the path in front of you, into the copse on your left. On your right, something moves on a dead tree and catches your eye. You lift your binoculars to see what it is, and there, perfectly framed in your lens, is a lesser spotted woodpecker – an increasingly rare little bird that you've wanted to see ever since you picked up your first bird book as an eight-year-old. 'NO WAY!' you cry out loud. In no time at all, the woodpecker has vanished, but in that moment, you have experienced absolute birding perfection, and a feeling of elation that you don't get from anything else.

This is going to happen to you. Not just this, but other moments like it. You just need to get outside and start birdwatching. Through birdwatching, you'll find a release from the oppression of depression. You'll see birds that you've never seen before and learn more about ones that you've seen plenty of times but never known their names. You'll meet amazing people and enjoy new friendships. You'll find wonderful places near home where you can escape and explore, and you'll be constantly surprised by what you find and where you find it.

Think of what happens when you go for a walk at the moment. You stare at the ground, lost in your destructive thoughts, don't you? But by discovering birdwatching, you'll learn to constantly look around and above you, and appreciate small things.

I'm going to describe another scene.

You're at a wetland nature reserve, where an exotic purple heron has been reported. You've found the part of the reserve where it's been seen, and you're in a hide, overlooking a marsh. What strikes you first is the noise – the cacophony of sound. It's like nothing you've ever heard before. Out there in the warm sunshine are hundreds of marsh frogs cackling away. And then a fellow birdwatcher in the hide points out the heron, sticking its head up from a ditch. What a bird it is! Surely it would be more at home in the south of France than here. On a high, you enjoy a day exploring the reserve in the midst of a spring heatwave, soaking up the sun and the birdsong, finding different species at every turn, and savouring the dazzling yellow of the yellow wagtails bobbing along the reservoir wall.

You start to recognise the good it's doing you. You know that you've enjoyed a kind of mindfulness that you can only get by getting out into nature – a thoroughly immersive experience for all the senses. Those experiences become etched in your memory for you to recall another time.

You'll find your spirits can be lifted by your first water rail stepping out of a reed bed in full view on a grey day, or a nuthatch suddenly dropping down from a tree in the park. You'll discover you can become absolutely absorbed in the pursuit of a rare bird or in watching a familiar wren or goldfinch in the garden.

You'll become lost in the moment, only realising some time after emerging from your bird-induced trance that you'd forgotten your troubles for a while. Your fizzing brain has been calmed for a few precious moments, and the burning destruction of your poisonous thoughts has been extinguished by something pure and joyous. It can't 'cure' your depression and anxiety by itself, but these positive experiences and feelings add up to slowly weaken their powers.

It might seem impossible to fit it into your life right now, but trust me, you'll find a way – and that's not just me saying that. Your counsellor will suggest finding time to do something you really enjoy, and this may be it. The main thing is that you recognise this is something you need to do, something that is good for you.

It's something you can add to your weaponry whenever you feel the darkness growing, something that can energise you when lethargy possesses your mind and body.

Birdwatching can't heal you on its own, but what it can do is bring excitement, joy and – at the very least – a bit of positive distraction back into your world.

SINGING

Ruth Routledge

Looking back now, nearly nine years and two children later, it's very obvious that I was suffering with postnatal depression, but at the time I didn't have a clue.

It didn't cross my mind to seek help, to try to do anything about it myself, or even to talk to anyone about how I was feeling. And that is the really hard thing about something like depression: the way it creeps up on you and lassoes you into a downward spiral of negative thoughts and behaviours which feed on each other and drive you steadily down. Couple that with your body having gone through the trauma of pregnancy, birth and breastfeeding, and your brain being a mush of sleep-deprived, hormone-infested, first-time-parent stress, I wonder that every first-time mum doesn't suffer from postnatal depression of some sort or another.

I would wake up in the morning feeling despondent, as though everything I was living and experiencing was through a grey filter. I would drag myself out of bed and go through the motions of looking after the baby, but feeling isolated from her. I was feeding and changing her, but not able to enjoy her smiles and laughter or feel motherly pride when she reached a new milestone. I avoided going out and meeting people. I felt so desperately lonely and had become so accustomed to feeling that way that going to meet people I didn't know well and having to make small talk felt impossibly daunting.

So how did I get through it? Well, I started a choir for parents where they could bring their babies.

Singing with others predates even language in evolutionary terms. It is a deep way of sharing an experience and communicating with others in a non-verbal way, resulting in a feeling of togetherness and even euphoria. Research has shown that when people sing together, their heartbeats become synchronised,[1] demonstrating that this experience of togetherness isn't just sharing

---

1 Vickhoff, B., Malmgren, H., Åström, R., Nyberg, G. *et al.* (2013) 'Music structure determines heart rate variability of singers.' *Frontiers in Psychology.* Accessed on 13/5/2020 at www.frontiersin.org/articles/10.3389/fpsyg.2013.00334/full.

an experience – it goes down to a deep physical level. I think this explains how singing together helps combat the loneliness, isolation and disconnectedness I describe. Without even knowing each other's names, we can learn a song together and experience this deep, heartbeat-level connection. And in my experience, having had this shared experience, we feel more at ease with each other and able to connect in a conversation.

For me, there is also something very different to singing in a group from singing on your own – in the shower, for example. Obviously, in the shower you are alone to let rip, but in a group there is another important factor: you are *listening and being heard*. I think this is a profound aspect of choir singing and a big clue to its benefits.

Our deepest feelings and emotions can be hard to articulate, especially when they are negative, or contrary to our expectations. There is so much pressure to feel joy at the birth of your child that you feel as though you are only allowed to feel happiness and fulfilment. My singing is a means of expression, which channels deep emotions in a cathartic way, without even having to consciously state them.

The act of singing a song – inhaling, vocalising with lyrics and melody on the exhalation, then repeating – is in itself an act of mindfulness.

POTTERY

Felicity Jacques-Diwani

Pottery saved my life. Well, that's a little dramatic. It would probably be more accurate to say pottery gave me life.

I am so fortunate in so many ways. Before pottery I had everything I ever wanted – a handsome husband, two beautiful children, lived in a place I loved, owned my house outright – but I felt empty. I felt as if I was hanging off the edge of a cliff by my fingernails, I felt as if my soul was dead. I was not OK and was constantly on the verge of tears.

A survivor of child sexual abuse and teenage rape, I've suffered from depression, anxiety, post-traumatic stress disorder (PTSD) and various eating disorders ever since I can remember. The first time I tried to kill myself, I was 13. I do not remember ever feeling at peace or happy.

Then 20 months ago, on a whim, I decided to take a pottery class. My children were both in school, and I've never really been able to work, so I was looking for something to do.

I've always felt very creative, but never had the confidence to be creative. I always loved art, I always loved to decorate, and I've always loved combining different colours.

I would take dolls and make them into punk rockers, using only safety pins, black fabric, black marker pen and a pair of scissors. I tore up magazines and covered everything in collage. I would make statement pieces with CD cases and hypodermic needles, saying things like 'not weird, just different'.

All the time I was told, 'No, you can't do art because you can't draw.' I have a natural shake in my hands; it affects me to the extent that I have no consistency in my hand control. Every letter I write will look different every time I write it. So, I can't classically draw or paint. I felt cheated.

It wasn't until I took this first pottery class that I realised being creative is not just about being able to paint a picture that other people found pleasing. Being creative is about using my imagination, something I have always had a lot of. I don't know if it was as an escape from my difficult childhood, but I exercised my imagination muscle constantly. My imagination could join a body-building competition and not look out of place. Being creative doesn't have to be freehand; being creative can be built from a foundation.

Discovering clay was a revelation. Clay is incredible. It is essentially mud, but with some manipulation and some heat it can turn into something beautiful, hard and permanent. Cover it in powdered glass and heat to an even higher temperature and it becomes smooth, glossy and colourful. Ceramics are everywhere. You can use them to eat and drink from, to cook with, to decorate, to protect and build with – they are even used in your hair straighteners.

Pottery is 50 per cent art, 50 per cent chemistry and 50 per cent pure luck (yes, I know). It teaches you, despite all the time and care you put into an item, not to get too attached, because any number of things can affect the outcome and cause it to crack or turn into a mess. You have to let go of control and go with the flow.

About a year ago I decided to take over my kids' playroom. It was just being used as giant experimental petri dish anyway. So I turned it into *my* playroom. My 'clay room'. I painted it white, so my mind wouldn't be distracted from what I was making. I installed a sink. I crowdfunded for a second hand kiln, which I set up in my garage, next to the screen wash, boxes of Christmas decorations, kids' bikes, skateboards, etc.

I watched endless YouTube videos on how to use a kiln, how to glaze, how to make a mug from a slab of clay. I joined many Facebook pottery groups and mined them for information. I set up an Instagram account to document my progress, and to get inspiration from established potters. I experimented. Some experiments came out incredible, some were just useable, and others were a complete disaster, but each item was a lesson, good or bad.

Often people say that conventional mindfulness is not always suitable for abuse or rape victims as it can sometimes be triggering for them when concentrating on parts of the body. So pottery is my mindfulness.

I lock myself in my studio, put on a podcast or my latest favourite album, and I focus totally on what I am creating with my hands. The feel of the clay, how squishy it is (and I'm not going to lie, the squishiness of clay is a huge attraction to me), the different stages of it as it dries. There is a race against time with clay because it dries out, although you do need it to dry out a bit so you can do certain things to it. Working in stages teaches me to have patience and slow down, but also have some sense of urgency. Everything is in balance. Yin and yang.

In my studio I get to create whatever I want; it is my space, it is my haven. I get to be the artist I always needed to be. I get to make pretty things that I see other people using every day, and it makes me happy that it makes them happy. I decorate the bottoms of my mugs, because it is an area other people see when you drink out of them. It's another excuse for me to add colour and shapes into the world.

I have been able to come off a lot of my mental health medication, but I'm certainly not cured by any means. I don't just have good days and bad days; I have good minutes and bad minutes. I now work around my children and when my mental illness will allow. Even if I just get half an hour in my studio a day, it helps clear my mind.

I sell what I make on the internet and the occasional craft fair. It gives me so much joy when someone else loves one of my pieces. But I still have the fear that maybe what I'm doing is dreadful; it's the eternal self-doubt, backed up by my school telling me all those years ago that I wasn't good enough. Then a customer emails me to tell me that the mug they bought is their favourite mug, the best they have ever had, and that's a huge boost to my self-confidence.

Pottery has given me pride in myself; it has given me a thing to wake up for in the morning.

It's given me passion.

It's given me life.

ART

Orna

There is one night, in your room, when you think, 'I can't do this', and you find yourself searching feverishly for a belt. You might just pass out very slowly, you think. But you can't find a belt, so you go to bed instead, and in the morning, you cry, but you draw something. 'Well,' you think, in a kind of simple literality, 'I wouldn't have been able to do that if I was dead.'

Depression brings with it a new kind of normalcy. Days are spent in a kind of chronic aloneness that no amount of smiling from strangers can pierce. You put on a cute outfit and do your hair, and you walk the dog, and wander the streets alone, pretending to be just as alive as anyone else, sometimes sitting in a bus stop, overwhelmed by all the crushing, violent nothing inhabiting your days.

You listen to music, the same songs on repeat, and you're so ashamed of yourself. You ask the air around you – dense and filled with the breath and sweat of the productive, the talented, and the employed, leaving wraith-like impressions as they pass you by – 'What happened to me? Where did I go?'

So, you go home again, but you learn to draw, and you're good at it. You hate admitting you are good at anything – this is not something you often feel – but (say it) you are good at it.

You follow YouTube tutorials, and mimic the sketches of Instagrammers you like, and you learn to draw, and yes, you realise, you're good at it. No one and nothing can take that feeling away.

You steadily shrink in the mirror, but when you draw, it's not a compulsion that bends you, but desire. You feel things you haven't felt in what seems like years: pride, a sense of achievement, of accomplishment, delight in combining paint and ether to effect a small change in this world, bright and flat and heartening.

You experiment with new and different tools, and when things are bad, it's art that allows you the space to be the person you have become. It's someone you neither like nor recognise – quiet, and focused, and lonely – but simply are, now. Art quietens your fears, and lets you be yourself without judgement. You are not crazy, or fat, or over-sensitive, or stupid; you are simple when you draw – two hands, black pens, white paper. You are at peace.

'I am in pain,' you tell your heart. 'I know,' it whispers, low and dark in your chest. But you like drawing; it soothes. You are not in pain in this moment.

Art therapy is a conduit for emotion – a way for those ill-equipped with words to represent their experience on a page. That's not your intention, but you're as elementary as you are complex (you're human) and your pictures are often studies of pain. They are of monsters escaping like vapour from the chest of a woman; of dark-eyed women drowning, of women broken and cut into segments like oranges, of women lying supine, reaching and gazing backwards with a pleading look; of a black figure in silhouette, calmly swinging beneath the waves, entangled in the tendrils of a massive stinging jellyfish.

Art saves you on a cold night in January. You have escaped all the badness, you think, in this fresh start, and you are at the kitchen table in your own country, with the cool hardwood of your mother's dining chairs supporting your back like a second spine.

'I'll do something with this,' you think – so you enter a competition, and you set up a little shop, and you ring other illustrators for advice, and you write an article about art therapy where your interviewees tell you the point of art therapy is not to be good, but to recover.

'It doesn't matter if it looks like a horse,' they say. 'What matters is that the creator knows it is a horse.' 'When did being good become more important than the process?' you wonder.

So, you stop. You wake up one morning, and you draw nothing. You don't draw for a whole month, and that month becomes two. You listen to the soft animal of your body when it begs you to be alone, and quiet. It has taken you over six months, but one day, you stay in bed all day and do nothing – no drawing, no talking, no TV – and you don't judge yourself for it.

But the paper is there, and when you are packing for a holiday with a friend, you think about the way you would like to spend your free time, and you realise you miss it, keenly.

In the kitchen, on the first night of your holiday on a Grecian party island, you forego bright lights, cheesy come-ons and spilled drinks, and you and your friend paint, quietly. You delight in his enjoyment and pride, and you realise that you are enjoying the smooth movements of the brush, so much.

There is pain there, too – there is always the same nugget of pain there. It will always be there, you realise. You grieve for the version of you that would once have much preferred the call of a dance floor, the drunken blather of a chat with a stranger, the excitement of the new and loud and garish.

But that pain lives in you now beside more grace, and compassion, and love. It is as much a part of you as your heart, or your hands.

With smooth, flowing movements, you acknowledge it, but stop fighting, and let it pass you by. You forgive yourself, and let go of where you might be, or what you should be.

You think of your first rudimentary pieces, and how different they were to what you're producing now, but realise that every piece was valid; every time you drew, you knew it was a horse. Like the discarded sheets around you, you are a work in progress: always learning, heart and hands.

MEDITATION

Charles

Feeling great being well. Feeling great being well. May you be well, may you be happy. May you be well, may you be happy.

Over the past 40 years these simple phrases have become my mantra. These 24 words have helped me bring a smile to my inside when I've needed it most, and provided me with a quick fix, a foot on the brakes when things start sliding downhill. The repetition and visualisation that goes along with this focus on the present moment, the idea of sharing something good and an underlying feeling of inter-connectedness that I get from this quick fix considerably lifts my spirits.

This mantra-based meditative mind hack is a contraction of a much deeper and wider traditional technique. For a number of years, the full thing, called Metta Bhavana – Loving Kindness – was my main meditation practice. At first it gave me an insight, then an even deeper insight, into how connected I was with everything and everyone around me. Beneath the abbreviated practice (those 24 words from the opening paragraph repeated over and over and over again, that I now use when things get difficult), lie years and years of focusing on my breath and studying a method of posture and movement training called tai chi chuan.

I'll admit it can be a struggle during the slumps, summoning the effort to sit still for five or ten or 20 minutes, or to coordinate all those arms and legs, but like some sort of perpetual motion machine, working with the body and the breath during my depressive episodes tends to lead to a desire to do more internal work. And the more you work with your breathing and body awareness, the more centred you become, reinforcing the positive effects of what you're doing, again increasing the desire to do more.

Whether I'm sitting or standing, still or moving, the

engagement of the mind on something fixed and constant, such as a mantra or a series of postures, keeps me here and now, in the present. And if I'm here in the present, I'm not worrying about the future or picking over the past, so I get the opportunity to become (however temporarily) calm and collected. When engaged in any of these meditational activities, I always find myself smiling and feeling good as the stresses and strains of everyday existence fall into perspective and then fade away completely.

By the way, this feeling does not come from thinking about the practices or worrying about getting them right, but from absorption in the practices themselves, in their performance, so to speak. And at the root of them all – yoga, Pilates, meditation, tai chi, qigong and so on and so forth – is the breath.

Learning to regulate and control the breath is the gateway to meditation and underpins just about any tradition you care to mention, from psychedelic shamanism to corporate mindfulness seminars. Like a fisherman focused on his float or the tip of his rod, the fierce attention that arises over time gives rise to a feeling of just being here, a feeling that can be not just soothing but at times exhilarating.

By turning my mind away from the tangled web of cares that hold me down and which can be exhausting even in people with good resilience, just being there in that moment, in that task, with that extraordinary focus, brings deep relaxation. And what's more, with a little experience it starts to bring renewed energy and vigour. The ability to do something when the ice starts to crack under my feet and I start sinking into the cold waters of depression feels nothing short of miraculous.

Anxiety and worry are exhausting. There is a physical tension that goes along with them that disturbs sleep and eventually wears one down. Whether from the perspective of Western science or Chinese medicine, stress kills. Meditation, be it seated or standing or moving (like the tai chi mentioned previously, or running, or yoga, or hula hoop – the activity isn't really the important factor), teaches us that we have the ability to release this tension we all carry, the stress bending us literally and metaphorically out of shape. And releasing stress from the body also seems to release it from the mind, or perhaps it's the other way around. Does it really matter, so long as it works?

There is a phrase used by some meditation teachers – 'thinking about not thinking' – and that really is what it's all about – just being. Sitting, standing, moving and just being with your body and mind and breath dancing together, trying to achieve some sort of union.

Feeling great being well.

May you be well, may you be happy.

KNITTING

Nicola Rossall

There is something about the act of knitting that puts me back in touch with my body and grounds me.

When my mental health started to deteriorate, I'd been running on empty for a long time. I'd withdrawn from the things that made me happy and had stopped exercising, socialising or having any hobbies. I was struggling to get out of bed, having a panic attack before leaving the house most mornings, holding myself together at work and then getting home and collapsing back into bed. I felt as if I'd lost myself and I didn't have a compass or a map to help me get back to safety.

Depression feels like an absence to me; it's an absence of joy, energy, pleasure, engagement, self-compassion, connection, motivation and more. I felt like a burnt-out shell; I felt wretched but wasn't able to cry or let out the emotions tangled up in me.

After a week of being on antidepressants, I met a friend

for lunch and walked past a yarn shop. The shelves and baskets of yarn captured my attention and I absorbed the different shades, textures and colour combinations. For the first time in months I engaged my senses, looked at and touched the yarn, and was fully in the moment.

I spent that whole evening knitting and figuring out basic stitches. There was something about the repetition that felt soothing for the first time in over a year. I was engrossed in something and it didn't feel forced or hard. I was clumsy and slow, but I managed it and every stitch felt like an achievement.

Over that weekend I made two hats and felt so proud of myself. When I look at them now, they seem so crude and basic, but still they represent progress and achievement to me. The ability to create something overcame some of the sense of failure that depression had forced on to me. There was something about knitting that worked for me. When I couldn't drag myself out of bed and get dressed, I could still knit. Even one stitch was progress, and once I'd started, I always wanted to do more. It allowed me to concentrate but didn't overwhelm me. I could also see tangible progress; I was getting quicker and neater and had started to understand what the yarn was doing by touch as well as sight.

Knitting uses up enough attention to enable me to focus on the present. I can feel the texture of the yarn on my fingers, hear the soothing click of the needles and watch the fabric slowly grow. It gently quietens my mind when it races. For me, there's something about the gentle repetition that helps enormously. If my mind spirals too far away from my knitting, I make mistakes, so the act of knitting brings me back to the present moment.

I have always done a lot of my best thinking by going for a walk, and knitting seems to provide a very similar experience. I am occupied by it, but enough of my mind is free to work through things. Starting a new row of stitches is like turning a corner; it's a chance to pause and consolidate. To me, knitting and walking provide the same sort of feedback loop; my body and brain are connected, and I can slow my thoughts down to a manageable pace and spur them into motion if I need to. Knitting provides a rhythm and a cadence that help me work through my thoughts and emotions.

The act of knitting clothes also has had a powerful effect on how I view my body. I want to make something that honours my body, fits well and makes me feel good. The cycle of self-loathing and punishment has been broken.

Knitting is a thing I do to be mindful. The soothing repetition and the sensation of manipulating the yarn and needles with my fingers feels so good. It calms my anxiety, and when I am knitting, I feel centred and present. When I knit, I need to focus on the present, and although my thoughts will start to wander, they don't spiral out of control or overwhelm me. If I lose myself in my thoughts, I make mistakes, and have to bring my thoughts back to my knitting.

The sense of achievement I get from creating something with my own hands provides affirmation. When I'm having a dark day, I look at the things I've made and remind myself what I'm capable of. Knitting gives me inspiration and energy and a place to reflect and find my authentic self.

If you are considering knitting, visit your local yarn shop and speak to the people in there or find a local knitting group. Remember, the internet and YouTube are your friends; watch videos of people knitting and find patterns online.

Kintsugi is a Japanese art form where broken pottery is repaired using gold. The fractures and scars in a pot become something beautiful and interesting. I'd like to think that yarn has been a bit like the powdered gold in a kintsugi pot for me. Yarn has helped me put myself back together. I'm a different person and I've gained wisdom and self-compassion on the way. I'm developing my authentic self and knitting is part of the jigsaw. Recovery for me is evolution.

GARDENING

Elisabeth Basford

It was late September and my brother, Sean, had been dead for over nine months. The shops had started to put out their Christmas decorations. I suddenly felt as though an immense black cloud had decided to land on my back. I could physically feel its weight, as the tears started to pour down my face. I stood there unable to move for about ten minutes.

Over the next few days, I struggled to do the simplest of tasks. Getting myself out of bed and dressed suddenly became a monumental task equivalent to climbing a mountain. I stopped doing everything and I could not even muster the energy needed to care for myself, let alone my children.

My husband made me an appointment to see the GP. His office was full of artworks, photos of his garden and perfectly arranged books on a variety of artists. I found it hard to look at the doctor as there was so much else to look at. I explained what had happened and how I couldn't even get out of bed now. His response shocked me.

'Well, if you can't get out of bed, don't. If you can't get ready, don't. Just give in to it.' I found this advice unusual given that I expected him to just tell me to snap out of it.

'Do you have a garden?' he suddenly asked.

'Well, yes but we haven't done much with it. We live in a new build.'

He then proceeded to show me photos of his garden, which looked beautiful. It was blooming but still incredibly ordered.

'A few years ago, I felt just like you,' he explained. 'Then I discovered gardening and it all changed. You see, you have depression and we can help you with some medication. But it will really help you to do something physical as well.'

I paid little attention. I wanted just to take the medication and hope that it would magic it away.

Over the next few days, I did exactly as I had been told. If I needed to stay in bed, then I would. The tablets seemed to be taking forever to work and I still had no energy to do anything. But after a couple of weeks, my husband suggested a trip to the garden centre to buy some plants for the garden. While there, I started talking to the owner who advised against putting in any plants until we had prepared the soil.

So, spurred on by her enthusiasm and advice, over the next few days I started digging with my husband. A good spell in the garden made me sweat, and I could feel my mood beginning to lift as endorphins were released. It started to become highly addictive. I'd always needed to force myself to get in the garden, but once I did, I could feel my spirits lifting the more I sweated.

Over the next few months I began to add shape to my garden. The more I gardened, the less I worried. Instead of lying awake all night petrified of my death, I'd lie there thinking up new creative ideas for my garden. I'd research plants by poring over books. And thus it was that as the garden started to take shape and blossom, so my own mental health started to recover, and I felt less and less depressed. I genuinely felt that I had found my purpose in life and something that I could truly excel in.

Gardening is a great form of exercise and there has been a lot research about the benefits of exercise. There is the lifting, the bending down, the digging, the raking, the carrying, etc. All of this can help you to develop quite a sweat. It's also far more interesting than going on gym equipment, because you can see a result. The right exercise for the individual can also serve as a distraction, enabling escape from the cycle of negative thoughts that encourage depression.

As I started to recover, I would still go and see my doctor regularly as he had requested, and the more I saw him, the more my mood seemed to have changed. By the final visit we spent much of the time sharing gardening tips and advice.

My story shows that there is no magic instant cure for depression. Recovery takes a great deal of time. It is also vital to adopt a multi-pronged method for fighting depression.

It is now over four years since I was diagnosed with depression. Now, I put on my gardening boots and gloves, turn on the radio and go and have a potter in the garden. It isn't long before I feel the balance of my mind restored. And on top of all that I have something beautiful to look at and admire, as I stand back and say, 'I made that.'

POETRY

Lorraine

Healing through poetry is how I survive.

Expressing my pain through words has always helped me as I experience awful periods of sadness, despair and hopelessness. I scribble in notebooks, on scraps of paper, and it's such a release for me to get my feelings out. Releasing pain in the form of poetry lessens its power and hold.

I started to write poetry in my teens; it was full of angst about the pain of unrequited love. I continued to write in my twenties and never would have imagined the power and freedom of expression poetry would give me, until a traumatic event changed my life for ever. My youngest sister, Siobhan (Von), died. She was one of my best friends, a treasured godmother, a wonderful sister. She was warm, intelligent, witty, funny and so kind. She was such a beautiful human being.

I remember not being able to read after Von died, which

really affected me, as reading is such a comforting distraction and means of escape, so I turned to the only constant which has kept me well throughout my life – writing and reading poetry.

Twelve days after my sister's death I sat down and wrote in a copybook how I felt. I didn't hold back. Often, I couldn't even see what I was writing as the tears were falling as fast as the ink was coming through the pen, but afterwards I felt a bit better. Being able to express my pain, mental anguish and the sheer magnitude of my loss helped in ways that I'm forever grateful for.

Sometimes, I journal with my poetry rather than using a computer. I love the physical act of handwriting and freely jotting down my thoughts and feelings. Seeing my words on a page, written by me, lessens their stronghold and impact. Then looking at these words as a reader forms a separation, putting the issue into context, de-magnifying it.

The very act of releasing sorrow in the form of a poem on to a page or screen is a transferral of emotion and pain that would have otherwise built up and resulted in serious mental health issues.

We all need support in many different forms, to connect and to feel valued and loved and practise more empathy. Expressing love, appreciation and support in equal measure is what makes us human. Poetry allows me to record my memories and lived experience, both happy and sad, life-changing and ordinary.

We all need a sense of purpose in the world; it's important to acknowledge this, and when I discovered that I could write good poetry, I realised it's the most wonderful gift I will ever own. I release my poems into the world for readers who I hope will discover and enjoy my work, and there's also a crucial letting go in that very act.

Recovery takes time and is a continual fluid process. There's no beginning and no end. I accept my feelings because they are mine and I know I have to deal with them as best I can.

As long as I can write it out, I know I'll be all right, secure in the knowledge that words can heal, quite like nothing else in this wonderful world.

COOKING

Ellen Kanner

In the throes of what I call a visit from the Crap Fairy, self-care can seem as impossible as DIY brain surgery. So does all the well-meaning advice people feel free to give, including, um, this. But there's one act of self-care you're already doing. Chances are, you're going to eat something today. And that is a wonderful thing. That's your own life force talking. So listen to it and let's build on that.

Happiness starts from within us. We may feel it in our hearts, but it really begins in our bellies. Also called our microbiomes, our bellies have been proven to be our second brains, and they're super-smart. It turns out gut instinct is real. By feeding our microbiomes well, we can feed our own happiness.

What do microbiomes want? Fiber, the one element in our diet we need most and get least. Fiber feeds the good bacteria in our microbiomes. You can find fiber in fruits, vegetables, beans, nuts, seeds and whole grains. These foods are also high in folate, magnesium, zinc and vitamin D, the vitamins, minerals and amino acids linked to wellbeing. They're legal, abundant and available without a prescription. Think of these mild-mannered foods as superheroes of uplift in disguise.

Yes, you can just pick up a meal somewhere. It often seems the quick and easy option, but too often it's full of things your microbiome doesn't want. Nourishing yourself offers a deeper, richer experience. You deserve it. You need it. You know first-hand that managing depression takes real work. It can sap your energy, so even making it through a day can feel like a victory. So reward yourself.

Feeding yourself, nourishing yourself, doesn't require a culinary degree, fancy ingredients, pricy kitchen gear or a lot of time. You probably have 15 minutes. That's all it takes to make something that pleases you, body and soul, something you'll have made for yourself. That has real value. And it's cheaper than therapy. Actually, it *is* therapy. It's called culinary therapy, and it's a thing. Google it.

Culinary therapy involves mindfulness, the top wellness trend. So look at that: you're already trending. There are all kinds of ways to be mindful, but I like to bring it into the kitchen and at the table, because we all have the opportunity to eat. We often don't take advantage of this opportunity, especially in times of stress and sadness.

After my mother died, my grieving father, left to his own devices, would eat nothing but ice cream. It was sweet, cool, soft, comforting. It satisfied his craving of the moment, but I watched it deplete his body and spirit. I wish I could tell you what I ate. Honestly, it was such a dark time, I don't remember.

Mindfulness helped me find a way out. It powered up my microbiome and improved my state of mind. I felt stronger, more stable, able to make better choices. I felt more like the self I try to be. If, like my father, you and your food choices aren't on good speaking terms, mindfulness has been proven to help.

It starts before you take the first bite. Stock up and surround yourself with the foods that nourish you. Notice I talk about nourishment, not nutrition. The definition of nutrition can be shape-shifting – your doctor tells you one thing, your favorite health blog says another. But we each intuitively know how nourished feels. It's not just eating, it's being fed with love. It's receiving what you need from a world that suddenly reveals itself as a kinder place. A nourishing meal can redeem even a bad day. It can make you and your microbiome happy.

Even when I couldn't eat, I could cook. One of the reasons

I love it is that it lets me experience the pure physical beauty of fruits and vegetables up close and hands on. As I cared for my father, feeling the heft of a lemon, the curve of it in my hand, taking a minute to admire its sunny color, bringing it to my nose to inhale its zingy, spirit-lifting scent, seemed the one bright spot in a day, the only positive thing I could do for myself. Call it culinary therapy, mindfulness or playing with your food, it's all good. Bring all your senses into the kitchen.

Preparing food centers me and quiets the chatter in my head. It slows me down in the best way. Let it do the same for you – and more. Cooking puts you in charge. A home-cooked meal is empowering because you get to choose the exact ingredients you feed yourself. It's also an act of love, a nice thing in these crazy days. It's love you show yourself, the people you feed, and the ingredients you work with. They'll love you right back.

Let's try it together. Get a box of pasta, any shape, any kind – basic semolina pasta, gluten-free pasta, whole wheat pasta, keto-friendly pasta, whatever you like. It just needs to please and suit you.

Now cook it. Start by bringing a big pot of water to boil. Shake in some salt – a trick I learned from an Italian friend and pasta maker. When the water comes to a rolling, bubbling boil, add the pasta and let the magic happen. You only need to give it a stir now and then, so it doesn't get lonely. My favorite cheap thrill is breathing in the toasty smell of pasta as it cooks, listening to it speak as it simmers, feeling the gentle tickle of the steam on my face, surrendering to the warmth and comfort of it.

The package cooking directions give you guidelines, but they're only guidelines. Taste-test a few minutes before the instructions indicate. You want it truly *al dente*, so you bite into it. *Al dente* pasta is happy pasta. Gummy pasta may be less happy. But it's still good.

When it's done, drain the pasta, reserving some of the cooking water – another Italian trick. Take the same pot you've just emptied, put it back on the burner and add a tablespoon/15 milliliters of olive oil per 2 ounce/60 gram serving – just enough to hug the pasta. When the oil starts to shimmer with heat, add some chopped garlic, one clove per every two servings. Turn down the heat a little, give it a stir, just till it turns soft and golden – we're only talking a few minutes. Add a pinch of red pepper flakes. They add a little pleasant warmth to the pasta and contain capsicum, a natural anti-inflammatory agent, too.

Now add your pasta back to the pot and give everything a toss. Add a glug or two of the pasta water and mix it in. The water has some starchiness and heft from the pasta; it thickens with heat and, tossed with the pasta, creates a sort of sauce to coat everything well. Season with salt and pepper. Give it a taste. The strands of pasta should glisten with olive oil and have some zip from the garlic and pepper.

Bravo, you did it. You've just made a traditional Italian dish with a fancy name – *pasta aglio, olio e pepperoncino*. It's a handful of ingredients requiring minimal fuss and expense – it's much cheaper than what you'd get at a restaurant – that rewards you with a mouthful of *wow*. It's greater than the sum of its parts, a little something-from-nothing magic.

My father couldn't quit ice cream. And since it offered him some solace, I didn't cut off his supply. But I started preparing meals we could eat together, like this one. It's so simple, yet so satisfying, and can be fancied up any number of ways. Your microbiome will be extra happy if you choose whole grain pasta (it adds fiber, remember?). For a nourishment bonus, I'd add some spinach, a few bright green leaves, like a bird's fancy plumage. Toss in a few handfuls into the pot of pasta and give everything a gentle mix. The spinach wilts into the pasta without any special effort. It imparts a very mild flavor – a plus for my vegetable-hating dad – but helps feed your microbiome. Try adding other herbs and ingredients that please you. Make this *your* pasta.

What you eat matters. So does *how* you eat. Too often

in our busy lives, we're so distracted or dispirited that eating becomes automatic, solitary, joyless. You can eat out of the pot while standing up tomorrow. Today, take the care and attention you put into cooking and bring it to the table. Serve yourself. Spoon the pasta into a bowl or plate. Treat yourself like a special guest. Because you are.

Sit and get comfortable. Let the tension go. Pay attention to yourself. Feel the rhythm of your breath. Remind yourself you are OK, you are taking care of yourself. Take a moment to appreciate all the effort and intention that went into preparing this meal. Now take a bite.

Taste how bold basic flavors can be, how the mild grain of the pasta wakes up with the garlic, pepper and salt. Now go beyond tasting it. *Feel* it. Focus on the chewy strands in your mouth, lightly slicked and sauced. Simple as it is, this single meal is a never-to-be-lived-again experience, an opportunity for communion, with your food, with yourself. And if you can share it with someone you love, all the better. It's a little thing with big consequences.

Cooking and eating a home-cooked meal will not solve all the world's problems, but it can make them more manageable. You'll be treating yourself with loving kindness. You'll give your spirits and microbiome a boost. You'll gain more confidence in the kitchen. Once you feel confident there – or anywhere – it spills over into the rest of your life. You've got this.

Being present, being conscious doesn't take time out of your day; it adds more dimension to it. It enhances the experience of living. And it's a practice. The more you do it, the better you get. You can't always control what life throws at you, can't tell when the Crap Fairy will pay a visit. But you can always choose to nourish yourself. Doing so will help hasten the Crap Fairy on her way.

So thank yourself. The secret sauce in any recipe isn't aged balsamic vinegar or anything you can buy. It's what you bring. Gratitude makes everything you eat more delicious. It makes your life more delicious, too. It lifts your energy. You can't lose. All this and you get dinner, too.

DOGS

Kate

I never realise just how tense my body is, until I'm on the beach with my dog.

I never realise just how loud my own voice is inside my head, until I'm on the beach with my dog.

I don't notice how jumbled up and anxious I am, until I'm on the beach with my dog.

Then, over a matter of a few minutes, my body relaxes, my conscious mind is able to tell my subconscious mind to back off for a while and the anxiety dissolves out of my system entirely.

Today the sun is shining. It's early on Sunday morning and the tide is only halfway in. Where I live, it's so flat that the outgoing tide can leave a few hundred metres of sand. Which means that it also comes in pretty quickly, too. So this morning all the dog-walkers are out, meandering along the wide strip of sand, pebble pools and rivulets of running water gleaming in the sunshine before the waves gobble it all up for another 12 hours, leaving us confined to the coastal path.

The beach is a brilliant place to exercise dogs because the tides bring new smells every time they cover the sand, so the dogs have to get to know it all over again, every time they visit. Great stimulation for a dog. And for me too as storms mean the beach is in a constant state of flux, offering new sights every time I set foot on the sand.

I lived by the sea for over seven years before I was finally in a position to have a dog in my life full-time. In the first six months since I got her, I have been to the beach more times than I ever visited in the preceding seven, and what having a dog has done for my mood is nothing short of remarkable.

Having a dog is like having a child in that it's really hard work and extremely rewarding at the same time. Except that kids are allowed into most seaside cafés whereas we're left out in the pouring rain, trying to lick froth off our coffees before the wind whips it away!

I suffer from depression. Most of the time it's under control, but I really need to look after myself to keep it that way. I have to sleep well, exercise, eat right and reduce my stress levels. All of which are hard to do. The hardest for me, though, is to keep myself in contact with family and friends. Not a problem when I'm fine, but when I'm going through a bad dose of depression, talking to people is the last thing I want to do.

Before I got a dog, I could happily not see or speak to anyone in particular for days. I wouldn't answer the phone, would fob friends off with an excusatory text message and take to the sofa for days at a time. When I'm really bad, the anxiety and sense of worthlessness are so overwhelming that the mere thought of showering and dressing are just too much.

Since Nikita, my dog, came to stay, I've had only one truly horrible weekend. I was grieving over something lost and feeling a loneliness I hadn't known in years. But I know that if I hadn't had her, it would have been much worse and taken a lot longer to get over.

She had to be walked. I had to get out of the house and on to the beach. The sun shone, the sea sparkled. I felt as if I wanted to curl up into a ball and disappear; that doesn't change, but I do believe it passes more quickly because you're outside. You realise that the world is still turning and that you belong in it, instead of just bricking yourself up, mentally speaking, and hiding from a world that actually quite likes you, even if you're having a hard time liking yourself right now for no good reason. Even if you don't engage in a long conversation, there are still the cursory hellos and shy smiles with a fellow walker as your dog gets into a game of chase with theirs.

Nikita needs to be walked, mentally stimulated, played with and loved. In return, she plays with me, loves me back and keeps my head above water, psychologically speaking, without even knowing it.

If you're the type who suffers debilitating depression where you can't get out of bed for long periods, I'd only have a dog if there's someone else who can do the walking and looking after in the house too, because dogs are not our tool and they only work if the love and care is reciprocal.

But if you can afford it and don't mind being tied down by the velvet ropes that come with that much responsibility, then I can only recommend a dog as a great thing to have in your life.

They get you out of yourself, when it's the last thing you want but the very thing you need. They love you and need you to the point where, to them at least, you are the most important thing in the world. And as long as you can feel the same about them, then that is a marriage made in mental health heaven.

SEWING

Sue Arnott

Hello, my name is Sue and I suffer with bipolar affective disorder and anxiety, and I want to tell you how sewing has transformed my life.

It was during a particularly low mood following the birth of my first son that others around me became concerned about me and one friend suggested that we attend a local sewing class which offered a free creche place for our babies. I went along, frankly, for the respite the creche place promised, and I was not expecting to fall utterly and devotedly in love with sewing.

My friend managed a whole term of sewing and I stayed for 16 years. What I enjoyed about it and what helped me was the friendships I developed – a new set of people with their own needs – and I soon became firm friends with one lady, Ann, in particular – newly widowed and some 30 years my senior. We became close through sourcing sewing items and creating new projects together. This all took my mind off the depression that enveloped me, and gave me a purpose outside the family.

For me, sewing is about the sewing machine. I feel at one with my lovely machine, and just the rhythm of the foot pedal whirring away can calm my thoughts. Using my hands to guide the lovely fabrics that I've chosen to sew gives me a sense of purpose and I get pleasure from the accurate markings on my presser feet and guiding the fabric through.

Each sewing experience is different – the smoothness of the fabrics, the ribbons, buttons and zips that enhance the project, and soon after starting to sew you can lose yourself completely within the task to hand.

I sew for pleasure rather than necessity, so I have the luxury of choosing the type of project I undertake, but it's always about the fabric and the machine. A good sewing machine is worth the investment.

It's not all about the glamour of the sewing machine, though. First, fabrics and threads need to be sourced and prepared, pressed flat and interfacings applied – it all takes time, and when you are feeling low or anxious, the steady habit of preparation fills your mind and occupies your hands.

When you are feeling hyper or manic, such preparations

force you to slow the quickening thoughts. Then you begin creating your project. Piece by piece the fabrics are sewn, the seams trimmed and pressed, zips are inserted until finally you have a finished object. It doesn't matter whether it's a tailored garment or a simple drawstring bag – you hold it with pride.

With sewing being online so much these days, especially quilting, there is no need to go out if you feel you can't. These days I prefer to sew by myself, but I'm grateful to those classes all those years ago and to the tutor who taught me a useful, life-changing skill.

I'm lucky to have a sewing room in our house where I can leave out my machines and projects, but it's perfectly possible to sew from the kitchen or dining-room table; you really don't need that much space to begin with. But it's nice to have somewhere of your own where you can relax and enjoy sewing or just create disorder with threads and trimmings while you plan.

Start by seeing if there are any sewing clubs or classes nearby – check out local fabric shops, which often have customer noticeboards with details. If you are lucky to have a sewing machine, some classes will let you take it along to use, which gives you an opportunity to try out the features, functions and stitches you have. Either way, I'd recommend a 'sampler' – a piece of good cotton or crisp calico – and stitch a length of each stitch on your machine. This gives you a chance to judge if stitches can be used decoratively.

For me, sewing saved my sanity.

SINGING

Georgina Woolfrey

I sing everywhere: on my bike, at work and obviously in the shower. But the summer before my 27th birthday, I wasn't singing in the shower. I was crying while thinking of ways to kill myself. For six months, my optimistic, life-loving soul was hijacked by a force that took its place in the driving seat of my every thought: depression.

Goodness, joy and fun existed in a different world on the other side of a locked door. Depression has a cunning way of showing you all the bad in the world, hiding all the good, and then portraying this biased view as the truth. I couldn't understand how the people around me were so full of joy; I decided they must all be kidding themselves.

I dragged myself through the unbearably long days, pasting on the closest thing to a smile I could remember. I couldn't even remember the person I'd been for 27 years and I came to an undeniable conclusion: I was just shit.

I became an emotional black hole; I didn't and couldn't care about anything. I lost all my self-confidence because I couldn't even hold a conversation. I believed that I didn't deserve to be loved.

I tried various tactics to wrench my soul from depression's grasp, including blu-tacking life-affirming messages all over my wall. A few months later this had ripped the paint off the wall, but it didn't touch depression. But there was one activity with a voice loud enough to challenge depression's onslaught of insults: singing at choir.

Like a memory stirred, singing reminded me of the happier person I'd once been, and it was the closest I felt to being her. Choir opened a crack in the doorway into that elusive world of happiness I couldn't otherwise reach. It allowed the light from that forgotten place to stream in, and I basked in its heavenly glow.

Choir gave me a foot-hold on recovery; feeling just 'not awful' was a miracle in itself, which offered a glimmer of hope that I was heading towards the dizzy heights of 'OK'. Singing was something – the only thing – that I could consistently enjoy.

At the time it felt like magic, but I now see that the healing power of group singing is made of many elements; however, there is one constant which runs through every cause of depression like an underlying bassline: the absence of human connection.

In the daily grind of our lives, where we'd prefer an 'unexpected item in the bagging area' to interacting with a human till operator, and where we silently stand shoulder to armpit inside sweaty boxes that transport us across hostile cities, our sense of connection is as non-existent as the conversation with the human being next to us.

When was the last time you sang in a group? And why did you do it? Whether it's at a football match or a wedding, adding our voice to the singing of a group connects us to the people around us, throwing out melodic lifelines that entwine us at our deepest level.

In the most important ceremonies of our lives, we sing together. Like indigenous tribes that live according to the rituals of their ancestors, we mark life's milestones by uniting our voices in song. In times of intense emotion or mourning, when we are pulled deep into our human-ness and experience the rawness at our core, we sing together.

Human connection is the foundation of our survival. At its heart, choir is teamwork, without the rafts and bad coffee (but often with cake). It's a contribution to something greater. And if you want to know what it feels like to be in a room where your voice meets others in powerful harmony that makes the air thick with joy, making your hairs stand on end and your face burst into a smile, then you'll have to be there. Part of it.

To sing in a group is to build a kingdom with voices. It is to create, and it is to fill your mind with musical notes and dynamics and rhythm and lyrics so that depression is squeezed. The hell. Out.

To sing in a community is also to build life-long friendships. Choir is people coming together to pursue a mutual passion and it is also – literally every week – hilarious. And laughter is one of the most powerful antidotes to depression's venom. We laugh during the warm-up games that we love to pretend we hate, at geeky musical theatre in-jokes, and at even more geeky niche musical references that you feel like a god if you actually get. There is innuendo all over the shop (and every time there's a rod and chimney reference in Mary Poppins), and stomach-shaking trying-not-to laughter when you realise you have absolutely no idea what you're supposed to be singing and catch someone's eye across the room. The camaraderie of oh-god-we-still-don't-know-it ten minutes before the final rehearsal, then huddling for a frantic run-through in the foyer. Immense pride when your friend sings solo for the first time.

I've kept coming to choir when house moves have meant

it's taken almost two hours to get there. I've stayed because those bonds, which have carried me when I've been down and lift me higher when I'm level, are stronger than depression. They pull me into the heart of something that is the backbone of our species' survival: community.

When you're depressed, self-destructive tendencies like ignoring your phone will disconnect you even more from friends and family. When my confidence and self-esteem were at rock bottom, 'fun' events just left me feeling worse, because they inevitably involved a situation that exposed my useless social skills. It became the sensible option to stop turning up. Choir kept me tethered to other humans, and the world.

Depression turned me against myself. I would seek out flaws in everything I did, compare myself with others, and constantly remind myself that I was crap at everything. And anxiety, depression's BFF, robbed me of the minimum focus I needed to do my job. At work, I felt utterly useless.

But at choir, I was forced to acknowledge that I wasn't useless at singing. I was actually quite good at it. And not only that, I was, we were, making progress week on week, completing more of a song, remembering more of the words, becoming more confident with the harmony. Progress by its nature leads to confidence, because it's the hard evidence of your ability that even depression can't deny.

My choir is one of the most cherished things in my life. Most choirs are non-audition, and a quick browse of their website will give you an idea of the vibe. If you're even mildly curious, contact some local choirs and ask if you can go along for a trial session. It's what I did... ten years (and 10,000 giggles) ago.

Choir has given me a sense of achievement that nothing else could. The power of getting that tricky part right and nailing the verse and chorus in spine-tingling harmony. Pride is transformative, and a rare gift when depression is doing everything in its power to steal it.

Choir can bring you comfort that even in your most wretched projection of the future, you will always have singing, and choir, and friends to sing with.

Depression bullied me into being quiet and meek because I didn't want to be seen for the hideous person I believed I was. Singing gives me a chance to raise my voice.

To anyone going through depression now, you will smile, and laugh, and love life again. And it might just be that group singing is the foot-hold you need to get yourself back.

FILMMAKING

Alice Evans

Following a severe breakdown at university at the age of 20, I continued to experience mental health problems. This has included some of the more dramatic and what doctors rather confusingly call 'positive' symptoms of schizophrenia, which are hallucinations and delusions, alongside the 'negative' symptoms including paralysing depression and lack of motivation. This has, in truth, been a serious nuisance in living the meaningful life that most people may take for granted.

I spent some years as what is termed 'a revolving door patient' of mental health services, coming on and off medication, which usually resulted in long stays in hospital or under the care of a crisis team. I was fortunate to gain enough understanding of my experiences to think about a long-term plan as to how I could create a meaningful life which would work alongside the experiences that have continued to affect me almost every day since my first breakdown at the age of 20.

During one of my longer hospital stays, I was encouraged to do some drawing, something I hadn't done since my childhood. I discovered, to my surprise, that it was very much a release from the difficult thoughts and feelings I was having. Encouraged by my doctor, after doing a local college course I applied for university.

My first day was terrifying. There were loads of new, seemingly super-confident, clever people and I felt I could hardly string a sentence together. However, I met a friend there who was super accepting of me and we remain firm friends. Eventually, I realised that all the crazy thoughts and ideas I had as part of my experiences could feed into the films and photographs I was making. Since then I have continued to make art, mostly short films, and I really believe that making films and artwork has had a huge part to play in helping me find meaning in what have been, at times, pretty difficult experiences.

Some people might be daunted by the idea of filmmaking as a way to manage a mental health condition. This might be because it could be seen to be expensive or a 'not for the likes of me' activity. However, I have found that making a short film is not as costly as you might think. Recently, whole feature films have been made on mobile phones, and new technologies relating to cameras have meant that shooting and editing films is easier and cheaper than ever before.

Similarly, some of the most creative films have been made by people with few or no resources because it forces you to be creative in problem solving and creating effects that would never appear in conventional studio-based films with a big budget. One film I made featured a lake of tinfoil, which was surprisingly effective and much more interesting than hiring a swimming pool or fancy set for the shoot.

The medium is accessible in a practical way and some of the quirks and glitches that come from making a film without a budget can mean that the overall effect is much more visually interesting and creatively rich than the latest Hollywood blockbuster.

Another advantage to filmmaking as a way to help manage mental health is that you can tell your own types of stories. Stories are very powerful things. They can help or hinder us in our daily lives.

Consider how stories are told and what they can reinforce about how we think about ourselves or others and our relationships to the world. Some of the stories surrounding those with mental health conditions can be very silly and unhelpful to those experiencing a mental health condition, perpetuating clichés, stigma and bias, whereas other stories can be empowering and challenge stereotypes.

Conventional filmmaking doesn't always appeal, as it seems to tell stories that don't relate to my experiences. Everything is so neatly explained that it doesn't always relate to the way I experience life. There are still some particularly ridiculous portrayals of mental illness, which don't represent the actual experience at all. They make people with mental health problems seem alien rather than human.

When I'm unwell, I find it very difficult to watch much in the way of films at the cinema or on TV. This is partly because I find them rather formulaic or clichéd, also because I experience visual and audio hallucinations which sometimes make it difficult to concentrate or sit still for long. I often walk out of the cinema after the first few minutes. This doesn't stop me making my own films, however; I don't have to see or listen to lots of other films to have an understanding of how to tell stories. I find that watching clichéd nonsense narrows down my thinking rather than helping me understand humanity better.

Making my own films helps me to introduce new ways of looking at things or helps create unusual stories. It also gives an outlet for some of the ideas I have and gives them value when otherwise they might be dismissed.

I find it satisfying to allow these thoughts and ideas to emerge through my creative work rather than being stuck in my head. It's a great way of ousting ideas and images, and there is some good relief to be found when ideas or thoughts I may have been obsessing about can be released and used in a productive, creative way. Filmmaking also gives me control of the way stories are told, making me the writer of my own stories rather than experiencing stories being mediated by the same people in the same formula all the time. Making films has also helped with my mental health because the type of films I make enable me to celebrate new ways of looking at things, and this has also given me a good way to work and connect with others.

When I make films, I work with a cast of actors and a crew these days, but you don't really need anything particularly elaborate to tell a story. You can make films with almost no kit or actors. Through basic stop-motion animation, filming everyday events or using existing footage, you can still make really great pieces of work.

Learning to make films has taken a lot of work and quite a lot of time, effort and study, but it has been very satisfying. It is a wonderful process because it allows a creative purpose for my different way of being in the world. I now look at things with more satisfaction than I did before I found this creative means of connecting meaningfully with others.

MEDITATION

Cassy Nunan

The two Ms of mindfulness and meditation have sadly become something of a popular culture cliché, but for me they have been transformational.

Like many people who strive and struggle to manage major depression throughout their life, I've lived through a seemingly endless domino-like sequence of traumas, beginning in early childhood. But now, after learning a few hard-earned lessons, I think I'm getting somewhere.

Two years ago, I made a big uncertain decision to taper (very slowly) off antidepressants. This is not a decision for everybody, but it was necessary for me. During this period, I began to feel emotions I'd forgotten about with gusto, ranging through blissful joy, general contentedness and utterly devastating fear and grief.

To manage these fears, and the terror of being alone after I left my partner, I turned to meditation and mindfulness. It became clear that the best I could do was to try to manage how I respond to my emotions.

I have learned to gently attend to enormous emotions and dreadful fears without turning sideways into extreme anxiety or dangerous depression. I practice meditation daily, often many times, relying on it as I would a lifebuoy in a churning sea of uncertainty and fear. It can take time and diligence for relief to come, but eventually it does. The buoy holds and lulls me until I feel supported by the depth, serenity and constancy of the ocean. I land in my own depth.

Meditation and mindfulness offer no guarantee or safe-guard against tsunamis or inevitable tumbles into life's mysterious messiness. Yet these assure me that I can be OK – in an uncanny way – at least for a while.

CYCLING

Fatima

A few days ago I had an appointment with a coach who is helping me with my studies that I start in a few months. One question from him followed me throughout that day. How did I manage to be energised, to keep myself motivated without anyone's help while suffering from depression? I can easily answer this question. With cycling!

In the past it hasn't been easy for me. I have been in so much pain mentally and physically, so exhausted, that I couldn't get out of bed for months. I kept asking myself: how can I get out of this hopeless situation?

My therapist recommended that I go out for a walk at least once a day. So I set myself a goal: get out for at least 22 minutes. A mental challenge, but I had the entire day to prepare myself to get out. It started to work. When I went out, I realised that outside were my favourite birds (sandpipers and kingfishers) and I wanted to see them every day. I slowly progressed and started to appreciate every little step I made.

One day I was watching the Tour de France on television and the same person won the stage on almost the same day that I was present at a year ago. I took this is a sign and got my dusty road bike and I went for a short ride. I thought that if I can walk, I could ride too.

This first ride (almost two years ago now) was amazing – so I decided to set myself another goal to keep me motivated: doing my first alpine pass in less than two months. I now had something to focus on.

I was still very tired but I used the same tactic that I used for the walks. I accepted my exhaustion and rested while mentally preparing for the upcoming ride in the evening.

The day I completed my first alpine pass, I was really

proud of myself. I started to use a bicycle app to document my progress. Seeing my results was very helpful. But I needed a new goal to keep myself going. I kept riding during the winter to stay fit for joining my cycling club's evening rides in the spring. They were all much faster than me, but the regular training made me much stronger.

My next big goal was to do two cyclo-events and going to watch the Tour de France on a climb. I achieved them step by step and my goals became bigger and bigger.

Through cycling and setting myself goals, I found I can control my mental health better. Sometimes the bad thoughts still come, but I refocus my mind, I look at my goals pinned on my wall, I check them online or I just plan my next ride.

The moment I sit on my bike and do the first pedal stroke, my negative mood switches off. I start to feel myself and the surroundings. How are my legs today? How does the wind feel on my skin? My mind gets busy with observing the beauty around me or guessing the bird chants. Nature has many little surprises, and you can see the big and small changes of every season. But my main focus is on the ride. Depending on the daily goal, I pay attention to the velocity, heart rate, cadence, route and efficient pedal movement. Some days I try to ride really hard and on other days I just move my legs and enjoy the day. I even go out to intentionally get lost, as it occupies my mind to reorientate myself.

On my bike I am in the here and now. Not in the future which can cause me anxiety or in my painful past and depression, which has little to say during the actual ride. Then, afterwards, my muscles feel really good, I feel relaxed and it helps me to sleep. The more I go out on my bike and stay in this calm state, the more my mind learns to adapt it to my daily life.

Today, every ride has a purpose. It's either getting fit for races or/and doing fantastic unforgettable long hard rides. While I'm cycling, the negative depression thoughts happen very rarely now.

Cycling is the key in coping with my depression. It gives me self-confidence and has taught my mind another way of thinking.

MOUNTAINEERING

Sarah

During my darkest days of anxiety and depression, I felt unloved, a burden, unworthy, unwanted and that the world would be a better place without me. Additionally, I couldn't sleep properly, experienced panic attacks and suffered with self-hatred. The only thing I saw was an eternity of darkness.

I am writing this 14 years later and in a better place. During my recovery journey, I started to find solace in exercise and in the mountains. Mountaineering didn't just teach me to be the raw version of myself; it gave me much more to help me manage mental illness.

The mountains helped me to overcome panic attacks.

Panic attacks caused me to drop out of university and, consequently, I felt like a failure. When I didn't think it could get worse, I then couldn't leave the house through fear of being ill or having another panic attack. My mind was plagued with 'what if' scenarios. I stooped to the lowest point in my life and all I could think about was suicide.

As part of my therapy, I had disclosed that I wanted to climb mountains. Part of my homework was exposing myself gradually to this situation. After many months of preparation, the pinnacle of my panic attack therapy was on Grisedale Pike in the Lake District in England. I remember it as if it was yesterday.

The clouds were a mix of dark and light grey. I approached the last scramble section before the summit and then BAM, the sneaky little gremlin was there. It had its hands around my throat, was stirring the contents of my stomach, playing drums on my heart and brushing my mind with a feather duster, making it all fuzzy. The sounds of birds and the voice of my girlfriend seemed distant. How can something do all these things simultaneously? I became paralysed with fear. Panic had taken a grip on me.

Among the whirring fear, a thought emerged from the darkness: 'I've come so far, I don't want panic to rule my life.' I remembered what my therapist said: 'Panic will peak and then pass.' I just wanted to leave the situation, leave the mountain and get back to the car. I wanted to return to my safe place.

I had to force myself to go against my flight instincts.

I sat down with my face in my hands and waited. Sure enough, the panic began to subside, and once again I could hear the birds around me and the sound of my girlfriend's voice. I turned around and scurried to the top. I made it. Panic grabbed me, but I waited until it got bored and left. It did not beat me.

This was the start of my journey into a life in the mountains.

Then comes trust.

To be in the mountains, you need to trust yourself, your team and your equipment.

Throughout my life, there have been challenging and traumatic moments. I was physically assaulted by a peer, for example, who shot a ball bearing out of a hunting slingshot and the ball bearing hit my head. Doctors said if it had hit my temple or eye, I might have died. On several different occasions I was sexually assaulted, manipulated and lied to. Fortunately, I had a loving family, but nevertheless it was hard to trust anyone. My guard was always up and this fuelled my anxiety; I would always assume the worst and only wanted to rely on myself.

Mountaineering requires you to learn to trust in many different elements.

First you need to learn to trust your gear. Are my boots OK? Is my rucksack waterproof enough? Is my climbing harness, carabiner and rope going to hold me?

Then there is the direct human element. Is my team buddy or guide going to be able to safely guide me up and down the mountain? Or, in the event of an avalanche, can they locate and dig me out? Do I trust my own ability to do the same?

It was vital to start on less technical terrain and build experience slowly. As time goes on, you learn that people can be trusted. I now have a select group of people that I trust with my life in the mountains.

Once I overcame trust and panic issues, it became easier to practise mindfulness.

MINDFULNESS AND CONCENTRATION

Anxiety and depression in combination are the masters of making the mind race. It is incredibly difficult to concentrate; the mind is always elsewhere. In truth, it is a lot harder for anxiety and depression to collaborate and make the mind race about negative things when you're packing for an adventure, researching and planning a route, or hearing the birds tweeting, rivers flowing, the 'chink' sounds on the steel rope or the sound of skis scraping through the snow.

Mountaineering makes you concentrate on what you are doing, which provides a huge respite from anxiety and depression. Focusing on the elements and sensations around you helps you to practise mindfulness and decrease anxiety.

SELF-ESTEEM

Depression had a great way of making me feel worthless and feel as if people hated me because I hated myself. Anxiety would make me dwell on these thoughts and analyse every interaction with people. Anxiety would make me question 'Did I do that right?' 'Did I say something offensive to that person?' 'They must think I am horrible or ugly.'

Mountaineering taught me that I can achieve things as the raw version of myself. It taught me that I can effectively communicate and connect with team mates and the mountains. Mountaineering taught me that I can work in a team, learn new skills and be capable of using those skills. Learning these things put a crack in the negative self-belief that fuelled my depression and anxiety.

MEMORIES

Depression and anxiety made me concentrate on the negative things about myself and the negative things that people did to me. Mountaineering helped me to create positive memories and I can look back on these memories when I feel myself on a path to darkness.

PROBLEM SOLVING

My anxiety and depression were always as a result of traumatic events that happened, and these mental health problems created difficulties in my life. When you are in the mountains, things can happen that you didn't anticipate, such as a sudden change in the weather, a trail is washed away due to an avalanche or landslide, or you sprain an ankle. In these situations, you need to use the knowledge, equipment and tools you have to overcome these situations or make a decision to turn back. When I have a failed summit attempt, I ask myself why and what could be done differently.

Mountaineering has helped me to problem-solve in a logical manner; something that anxiety and depression often stop you from doing. You learn that it is OK to have good and bad days. I have had several failed summit attempts due to a combination of anxiety and weather conditions. Mountaineering taught me this is OK and not to be so hard on myself.

To this end, I do have relapses, but thanks to you, mountaineering, those relapses are never as gloomy as the darkest days that I previously experienced. I am able to draw on what I have learned to crack the foundations beneath anxiety and depression. Consequently, I am able to pull myself out of the hole quicker.

Recovery happens in small steps, so be patient with yourself. If you have an outdoor dream, research the shit out of it and go for it.

I promise you that it can get better. Most importantly, do what you enjoy.

HORSE RIDING

Niki

There is something about the outside of a horse that is good for the inside of a man. 'No hour of life is wasted that is spent in the saddle,' said Winston Churchill.

Churchill's notable quotation has been used regularly within the equine world, to the point that it has become a go-to for anyone trying to describe the freedom and joy that riding horses can bring. It's hard to improve on his eloquence, but as a writer and artist who has been diagnosed with depression, it is important for me to share my own experiences and how this quote has poignancy in relation to my mental health.

I returned to riding after an 18-year break, following the birth of my second son, having been diagnosed with depression and being hospitalised during my second year of studying for my art degree. I was, again, in a low place, with two children to look after, a failing marriage, a demanding teaching job and postnatal depression. I had slowly become isolated, introverted and inactive, losing a great deal of my creative impulse. This perpetuated my depression and it felt as if my situation was heading from bad to worse.

At the time my mum thought I needed something to focus on, something that would provide a new stimulus, regular routine and exercise. We talked at length about finding a horse to ride, something I thought I would never achieve again despite having ridden to a high level during my teens and early 20s, before going to art school. Horses are expensive animals to keep and require a big commitment. This was a worry, but I felt compelled to make changes and take the risk this presented. At that point in my life, things couldn't get any worse.

I believe good horses always seem to find you, that it's very hard to find *them*, and by luck a small, piebald horse named Wanda came our way. There began a relationship that has lasted for more than seven years. Wanda is, by nature, one of the most characterful horses I know. She enjoys human company and is highly inquisitive. Sometimes she is a complete diva (Wanda knows best) but she is one of the most reliable horses I've ridden. This reliability was refreshing, a feeling that I wasn't alone and had consistency and routine in my life. Before we brought her home, her previous owner said, 'Wanda will always see you right; she sucks up your worries and shows you how to relax and have faith in yourself.' This passing comment stayed in my mind and is probably the best summary of how our rider–horse relationship evolved.

Many riders get caught up in the day-to-day of horse ownership – the bills, keeping your horse well, over-coming glitches in your training, dark and cold days riding out in the winter. It's easy to overlook the positives; keeping horses is a lifestyle, a commitment. If you own a horse, it's not an activity you can pick up and put down. But this, in itself, began to have a positive impact on my own life. A reason to get up, get dressed, and get out there.

As I stepped into a routine, had daily activity, tasks to complete, an animal to care for, I felt as if I had direction. Being someone who had always been a 'high achiever', this was refreshing. I had new short-term, achievable goals, which were nothing to do with work and raising my children, and more about small steps towards build-ing a relationship with Wanda and having time on my own with her.

For the first few months we rode out most days – not

far, but round our family farm. I explored and revisited places that I hadn't been to since I was a teenager. The more I became engaged with the environment around me, the more I developed a new sense of adventure and enquiry.

The simple activity of exploring, seeing nature at a slower pace, from above, in more detail, helped me to slow down my mind. I began to appreciate micro detail, but also the 'bigger picture'. I noticed the change of seasons, how the weather had an impact of both my own and Wanda's mood, and how seasonal change marked time. Life became more stimulated and I was able to appreciate the world around me, and the part I play within the environment and the future I shared with it.

My partner, who also has depression, once said to me (when reflecting upon his down days), 'Silence is golden, but never silent.' This resonated with me. I have a very busy mind that rarely is quiet. I like my mind – it's fantastic, lively and exhausting all at the same time, making me the creative person I am. By planning ahead, timetabling my commitments and thinking about the future, I have found that I look after myself better, eat regularly and healthily, and my mood is kept a little more in check.

Riding, particularly alone and rurally, gives me the opportunity to clear my head and meditate. The regular motion of the horse, the tempo of gait and the thrill of moving at speed all help. Exercising myself, moving, and the work I need to put in to care for Wanda, the lifting, cleaning and tidying. All this provides clarity of mind, which has helped me to develop a new mindset for the way I see and understand my depression. I get the best 'silence' I can when I am engaging with horses.

But you don't need to own a horse to gain positive experiences. Local stables still offer riding lessons or trail riding. Many yards and organisations offer volunteer roles, including charities working with people with disabilities. Even inner cities have opportunities to ride. Something as simple as just interacting visually with these beautiful animals in a field when on a country walk can really help.

Through riding I have had the opportunity to develop a great support network of new friends, trainers, equine and human physiotherapists, personal trainers and performance coaches. With their support, I have travelled with Wanda, competing across the country and achieving more than I had ever expected. We have a close relationship, there is massive trust which I have learned to give, and together we have become older and maybe a little wiser.

I've learned that depression will never leave me but I still have what I call 'quieter days'. It can be hard to keep up with all the commitments in my life, but I have found that horse riding provides me with a structured time to reflect, be still, ground myself and also plan for the future.

I continue to take low-level medication, which I find helpful in managing anxiety. There is no doubt that horses have allowed me to see a world beyond depression, to explore who I am, my sense of self and place within the environment I live in and the detail and complexity of nature at a slower pace.

Reflecting back to Churchill and his prophetic thoughts – 'No hour of life is wasted that is spent in the saddle' – I think he was on to something. Although I'd like to paraphrase and suggest 'no hour of life is wasted that is spent around nature'.

When thinking about my own experiences, the links between nature, environment and riding have been the most pivotal to me in managing depression. Horse riding has helped me to explore this and it's something that I appreciate on a daily basis.

MINDFUL RUNNING

Rachel

A butterfly lands on the buddleia of a neighbour's front garden. I stop and inhale the sweet, floral scent as I watch her delicate wings beat against the first signs of summer. It provides a welcome opportunity to catch my breath because, no, I am not on a nature trail; I am on a run.

Three years ago, the idea of pausing during a run, let alone stopping to enjoy the sights and smells around me, would have felt like an alien concept.

I started running regularly because I'd signed up to do a 10K race with colleagues and hated the idea of being the slowest. I felt like the only solution was to train – and train hard – and for some unknown reason, I continued to pile this pressure on myself after the event had passed.

I ran with headphones in, head down and an app reminding me to speed up every 0.5 kilometres. I became borderline obsessed with viewing strangers' running data online, and if my speed or distance lagged behind theirs, I instantly felt like a failure.

Then I stumbled upon a mindful running podcast. Within 30 minutes, my entire understanding of exercise and its connection to our mental health had changed.

Mindful running is about being present while you pound the pavement. Instead of running to get fit, lose weight or achieve a new personal best, it's about fine-tuning your awareness of the environment around you, as well as your internal dialogue.

For me, this means noticing the changing light as the sun sets, enjoying the breeze against my skin and listening to the sounds of nature and human life as I run. There is nothing like marvelling at the world to put your problems into perspective.

It also means observing a negative thought attempting to creep into my consciousness – like that voice that says 'you're not good enough' or 'you should have done so-and-so by now' – acknowledging that thought, then letting it float away into the evening air.

I am a planner by nature and predisposed to worrying

about the future, rather than enjoying the present. But running helps me draw myself back to the here and now. When I feel my mind wander, I refocus on the reassuring rhythm of my steps: 'One two, one two, one two.'

Mindful running hasn't eradicated stress in my life, but it helps me to compartmentalise it, taming the beast into a more manageable species.

We all have mental health, we all have physical health, and it all exists on a spectrum. We might go to the gym or eat healthy foods to keep our bodies strong, but so many of us take our minds for granted. I certainly used to. But now, when I'm feeling stressed, anxious or over-whelmed, I pull on my trainers. Running provides my mind with much-needed nourishment, helping to build up mental resilience and enabling me to cope better when life throws its curveballs.

Without the pressure of speed when I run, I've also connected with people in the small suburb I call home; from the young mum who encouraged her daughter to high-five me when I got to the top of a hill, to the elderly woman who felt able to stop me for a chat, simply because I'd smiled and wished her a good morning. Former me would have unknowingly sprinted past. With loneliness and mental illness tangled like two insep-arable necklaces, these simple yet memorable human interactions can only be a good thing.

Sure, mindful running may seem a little hippy-dippy before you've tried it, but when I wrote an article about a year ago, it became clear that I'm far from the first person to reap its rewards. Hordes of people got in touch to tell me how ditching fitness trackers and running mindfully has helped them de-stress and finally enjoy exercise. One woman even said it helped her grieve after she lost her husband and daughter in quick succession.

The global wellness industry is worth an ever-increasing fortune. It feels as if every man and his dog are trying to sell us the latest product or programme to de-stress and improve our mental health and wellbeing. The biggest joy of mindful running? It's entirely free.

So give it a try. You might spot me gawping at a butterfly.

SURFING

Marigny Goodyear

I'm straddling my surfboard out past the breakers, watching the smooth, glassy water ripple from the falling raindrops drizzling down. The late September air has a bite to it, as if autumn is finally sinking its teeth in. I am lost in wonder at Mother Ocean's beauty.

I look up just in time to see a five-foot wall of water barreling toward me. There is no time to think. Instinctively, I turn and begin to paddle with all my might. I feel the pull of gravity and speed, as the wave picks me up and I slide down the face, leaning right and digging my inside rail into the wave. I glide up and down the face of the wave, and for just a few seconds, I am part of it.

Time is different in the ocean, and I realize that the perceived hour I've been in the water has actually stretched into three. It is these moments that I live for. In these three hours, I am at peace.

Peace. Not an easy thing for me to achieve. As one who

suffers from chronic stress and anxiety, peace is the goal that, most of the time, seems just out of reach. But not here. Not while Mother Ocean cradles me on her surface.

I've suffered from anxiety my entire life and have only been surfing for about ten years. It's hard for me to think of how I coped before Mother Ocean became my guide. Surfing has changed my life, and now many of my decisions are based on how and when I can get to the beach. Now that I've heard her call and listened to her guidance, I know there is no better way for me.

The moment that I step into the tide line and wade into the shallows, I am not thinking about anything but how to navigate through the white water. My mind does not wander past getting out beyond the shifty breaking waves, and once I'm out, I'm searching.

For that dark line on the horizon. For that little bump that is a smidge higher than the rest of the surface. Sometimes I don't see anything, but in my gut I feel a pull to the north, or south. I listen to that feeling. I trust myself in the water.

That is in stark contrast to the rest of my life, when I am constantly questioning, over-analyzing, and personalizing just about every little thing. On land, at any given moment I live in some state of overwhelm. The idea of a trip to the grocery store can bring me to tears. Managing a household's schedule makes my heartbeat race. Trying daily to succeed in my career can lead to a migraine.

I have trouble listening to my instincts on land. My gut says one thing and my head quickly tells me a conflicting story. Then my heart interjects with an emotional response and, pretty soon, I am living within a tornado. It's exhausting, and eventually causes me to collapse into a puddle on the floor.

But not here. Not now. For now, I am a mermaid. I am part of something larger than myself. The internal dialog is quickly forgotten and I am simply present.

The ocean teaches me many lessons. One of the biggest ones is adaptability. I am not in charge while in the sea. There is something much greater than myself calling the shots and I simply have to make decisions based on Mother Ocean's moods. I have to adapt to steep fast waves or mushy crumbly ones. When I'm on a wave, I must decide within a second what maneuvers to make based on the story that is being told right in front of me. Move up or down. Turn hard back into the powerful part of the wave, or get in front of it fast, before it closes out and swallows me whole.

When I paddle out, I look for rip tides and green water, to aid me in getting past the breakers. I don't get to decide where I want to paddle out. She tells me. Mother Ocean shows me the path of least resistance so I can preserve my energy for when I need it most. In this way, the ocean is my guide.

I surf a shifty beach break and so I can't stay in one place and hope a wave will magically come to me. I have to observe and move to where I will be best able to catch a ride. Also, I have to get the hell out the way when I see a larger than ordinary set out in the distance. I paddle as hard as I can out into deeper waters, hoping that I make it out far enough before the wave crashes down with mighty force.

Sometimes I make it. Sometimes I don't. In those times, I have to dive deep, let it come down on top of me, and, afterwards, scramble to the surface to take a quick breath before the next wave arrives and I have to dive deep once again. Occasionally, I get stuck and have to take five waves on the head. That's just Mother Ocean reminding me that she is in charge.

In my life on land, I struggle to retain control when I should simply let myself adapt to situations that are out of my control. After I surf, it is easier to achieve this. I can better welcome changing plans or unexpected expenses. When disappointment arrives, I find myself better able to accept it and move on rather than fixate, blame, and overthink.

The ocean also teaches me patience. As frothing as I might be for that long ride, I have to remember that it's not up to me. Sometimes, the waves sets are far apart – I mean, like 30 minutes apart – and I just have to wait.

Also, there might be too much wind to surf at all. Or maybe there are simply no waves that week. During these periods, I choose activities that will strengthen my body for the next time there is swell. I have to make the best of that time.

In land life, there are also lulls, and in those times I find I am particularly vulnerable to 'hamster wheel brain'. The hamster keeps on running and that wheel keeps on spinning, getting me nowhere but frustrated, antsy, and irritable.

It helps me to remember that, in those times, I can choose to engage in activities that will make me stronger for when the faster pace of life kicks in. Meditation and exercise are key for me in those moments, and help me to remember Mother Ocean's lessons.

Finally, the ocean often hands me a large dose of humility. In the morning, I can feel as if I'm surfing the best I have ever been able to in all my life. By afternoon, I may be struggling to catch waves or, if I do, to stay on them. In fact, it is common that when I get a superior feeling out in the line-up, chances are that a healthy smack in the face is not that far behind.

When this happens, regardless of me surfing poorly, I know that I've learned something that will help me next time. I try to think of this when I feel I've made a mistake at work or within my relationships. I attempt to take what I can learn, and apply it to future situations.

In fact, I have to remind myself that if I'm not having moments where I feel like a total kook, in the water or on land, that means I'm not trying anything new, and probably not growing. Stagnation is not a place where I'm comfortable.

Around the world, surfing has become a tool to calm anxiety and depression, treat PTSD, and help people with all sorts of emotional and psychological disorders. If you are inspired to get into the ocean, do so with caution and education. Look up teachers or schools that are closest to you. If you're a woman, I highly recommend searching out other women to coach you.

The ocean is unpredictable. Safety is always paramount, and surfing is not an activity that should be gone into blindly. Surfers may make it look easy, but, aside from raising a child, it is the hardest thing that I have ever learned to do in my life, and, by far, the most rewarding.

For me, surfing is my medicine. As I continue to learn and improve, the medicine gets stronger. I will never stop learning. I will always be listening to the lessons that Mother Ocean teaches. Her wisdom gets me through and, for that, I feel I've been given a gift. My gratitude stretches far and wide, and into her arms I go.

BIRDWATCHING

Matt

There is, thankfully, an increasing realisation that getting closer to nature can have a beneficial effect on mental health. And it makes sense. Appreciating the sheer beauty of even the humblest, most everyday species (a starling, say) helps to take us out of ourselves, even if only momentarily.

Seeing a bird like a swallow, and realising that it has flown halfway around the planet to get here, can give us a sense of being part of something much, much larger than ourselves and our own very real troubles, and a sense, too, of the world and the seasons continuing to turn regardless. And seeing any bird can be inspirational, or consolatory, or can, by association, make connections to memories of much happier times.

What doesn't get talked about enough, though, is the beneficial effect of the very process of birdwatching (which is my own preference, although you could just as easily substitute 'butterfly' or 'dragonfly' or 'mammal' for 'bird' in that sentence).

Let me explain. On the face of it, we're not that great at spending time alone, or at thinking about important life issues. But that, I suspect, is one reason why birdwatching is becoming so popular.

In short, it grants us permission to spend time alone with our thoughts, and to take our time in processing them, with the side benefit of providing a motivation to get out of the house and do something at least a little active. Maybe it's no coincidence that angling remains a hugely popular pastime, too.

In my mid-30s, I suffered a period of intense depression. It was a shock to me, because I'd never encountered it before, and although I suspected, right from the first moment that I realised I was depressed, that it was rooted in some very specific circumstances (a year earlier, my sister had died from cancer, aged 35), I was at a loss as to how to cope with it.

I had a certain amount of time off work, but financial necessity meant going back before I should have done. Fortunately, my job at the time involved a pretty unbending routine, and I drifted through the days there in a daze, doing things mechanically and without a great deal of thought, but getting through. In the evenings and at weekends, I lay on the sofa, unable to concentrate on reading or watching TV, or anything else, for that matter. Time seemed to both speed up and slow down. At times I'd realise I'd lain there for four or five hours doing absolutely nothing; at others the days would seem to grind to a halt mid-afternoon and stubbornly refuse to move on.

Now, admittedly, I was getting plenty of time alone to think, but the problem was that I couldn't bring myself to actually do it. I felt as though I was facing a massively high wall of repetitive, negative thoughts which I had no idea how to get over, or else I'd find my mind going completely blank.

That's where birdwatching came in. I'd been a birder as a child, had drifted away from it for a few years, then got back into it in my late 20s. Before the depression hit, I'd birdwatched regularly at weekends and on lighter evenings, and somewhere at the back of my mind was a nagging feeling that if I could just get out there with my binoculars again – even once – it might do me the world of good.

It was that part of spring when everything in the avian world is in motion, as winter visitors depart for Arctic breeding grounds and summer visitors start to arrive from all points south. Even many of what we think of as resident species are on the move from winter feeding grounds to breeding areas.

That opens up a much wider range of birds that you might potentially see, and so I set myself a target. A very small and pretty easy one, but a target nonetheless. I'd go out with the intention of finding a passage migrant (a bird that is just passing through the area on its way to its breeding grounds).

From home, I had to walk through the heart of my large industrial village. This was the hard bit. I didn't want to see anyone I knew; I didn't want to talk. I was constantly struggling with the desire to give in and turn around and get home to the sofa again, where life was at least simple in its emptiness.

But I carried on. By the time I reached the top of the steep hill out of the village, I was puffing and blowing, and my heart rate was up, but I had a tiny sense of achievement. I might as well go on now, I thought, so I carried on past the quarry and to the rocky outcrops and sheep pastures of the forest.

And I walked, and walked, and walked, without seeing anything other than the resident birds. But the very act of putting one foot in front of the other, again and again, brought a change. A medically trained person could tell me about the effects of endorphins being released into my body, but it was simpler than that, I think. It was more like a case of remembering that I was alive. Not just existing, but alive. This was what people did, I remembered. They walked, and breathed in and out, and cursed the rain that lashed them as vehemently as they praised the sunshine.

I'd turned toward home when I caught a flash of pure white in the last sheep field before the quarry. I focused the binoculars on it, and there it was – a pristine male wheatear, paused atop a hummock as it looked for insect prey. They're passage migrants, so that was my target ticked off. I felt a tiny but definite surge of satisfaction of having achieved a goal that, while entirely arbitrary, was accomplished through my own effort. For the first time in months, I felt as though I'd made something happen, rather than letting depression happen to me.

Wheatears are small birds a little bigger than a robin, with sharply defined grey, black, white and buff markings, and a strikingly white rump. They're among the very first of summer visitors to arrive, from the start of March, but their migration carries on until mid-May, as birds bound for Greenland and even northern Canada pass through the UK, having started out in sub-Saharan Africa. At all times, they have an air of robustness and busy activity, puffing their chests out against the world and getting on with business wherever they fetch up. You can imagine why it felt like a particularly good bird to see at that moment.

But there's one more thing about birdwatching that, I realised, helped me start to climb out of the trough of depression I'd fallen into, and that's that it slowly but steadily convinces you that good luck exists, even if it goes missing for long periods.

It was there in that encounter with the wheatear. For all that I was looking in a spot where they were likely to be, at the right time of year, I needed a bit of good fortune, too. The weather was just right. There were sheep in the field (always popular with wheatears because they attract insects). There weren't any dog-walkers passing by on the footpath while I was there. Five minutes either side of the sighting, the bird might have been in the further fields, or obscured by the sheep, or it might have moved on before I could see it. But it hadn't. Our paths had intersected, a perfect coincidence of time and space had occurred, and I had a small but significant reminder that the universe wasn't a malevolent force intent on inflicting misery on me. I walked home with the first unforced smile I'd had on my face for months.

Coming out of depression was a slow process, and I've slipped back in for lengthy periods on a couple of occasions, but birdwatching has helped me avoid it for long stretches, too, and to fight it when its onset has been unavoidable.

And it's the watching that's important, I know now. The birds themselves can play their part, of course, but the watching is the key. It offers time and space to think, valuable exercise, the chance to set manageable goals with small but significant rewards, and a sense that good luck exists alongside and in balance with bad luck.

It reminds me, unfailingly, that I'm alive.

NATURAL OPEN SPACES

Olivia

It happened like this.

I'm seven. Maybe eight. Funny thing, looking back, memory and story both fickle and malleable. I could have been five. But stuff had already happened; that much I know. I was already living in parts of my head that were shadowy, set to get darker as the years rolled on, set, already, to become the frightening, the unspeakable and the unreachable.

I am at the bottom of our garden in North London. It backed on to a train line, separated by a wire fence that, if no one was looking, I could climb, digging the toes of my buckled, sensible shoes into the handy, child-size-foot square mesh. If it was cold, the wire hurt my hands. From my vantage point halfway up, I clung on, body pressed against the fence, anxious and excited and just the right amount of scared; not of the height or the climb or the cold or the wire, but of the possibility that the Big Train might come at any minute – and that was a scary, scary thing for me then. But the best of all, the reason, the purpose of this climb-and-cling was what I could see. The faraway land that had trees, silhouetted, smoky grey-blue, a slither of field here and there, and, the longer I looked (or was it imagined?), hills, rolling into distance, space, beyondness. The calm and the awe, the bigness of it all soothed me like a balm, held me, talked to me of stuff bigger than me, further and wilder and more open than the closedness that was already encroaching, a claustrophobia born of who knows what stifling moments, indoors. In Doors. Not a good place.

It also happened like this.

My lovely godmother would appear at Christmas in a flurry of furs, face powder and heels. With the good sense of a mature and unmarried woman in the 1960s, she would bundle me up in thick clothes, warm, lip-sticky words and private cuddles. Taking me firmly by the hand, she'd march me to the park, just in time for me to hear, as we closed the big front door behind us, the harsh cacophony of my parents' Christmas rituals: shrieks, slams, stomps, shouts and recriminations – all left behind us as we, intrepid explorers, set off. At the park, the trees and the greens, the slopes and the lake banks would be tinged with iciness, the splendour of filigreed frost and, if we were lucky, a coating of snow. Best of all, there'd be the quiet, the space, the breathing of remaining leaves and the crackle of twigs underfoot.

It all spoke to me again, silently and wordlessly then, of beyondness, of More Than Me, of space and quiet, an elusive peace.

And then it happened like this.

I am 21. In the years between the wire fence and the park escapes, other darknesses. Nothing that'd kill you, don't get me wrong. But stuff that makes you shrink into yourself, makes the world shrink, too, around you. I had grown thorns like a porcupine, I was tensed and wired like a spring, and, looking back with compassion now at last, I want to unravel myself, stretch and soften that girl out in the sun and warmth and somehow say, 'It's OK.' My mind was trained on a nebulous fantasy of escape – in all and any form, mental obliteration and physical removal – and that removal at last took me, one night, after a series of other long stories, to a riverbank in India. And there I lay, at night – my first real encounter with a hugeness that surpasses all understanding, an openness and wildness, that, while wild and unknowable, nevertheless held me, reminding me that it was bigger than anything, would outlast all my trivia, would outdark my darkness and outlight my exuberances. That bigness didn't give a damn about me, not because it didn't care but because it didn't need to care; it surpassed all notions of caring, but therefore of judging and hurting, too. It did what it was intrinsically in its nature to do: be. I was awed. And I was hooked.

And it kept on happening. Through the jarring and the jolts, the plummets, soars and the grim, flat plateaux that make up the landscape of a life shared with bipolar, my escapes to natural open spaces continued to ground me and keep me. They have offered me sanctuary, excitement, wonder. They held and hold out expanse of mind when mine is shrinking, meaning when there seems to be none, tunes in a discordant time, words when speech eluded me, colours in a grey miasma, textures when I could feel nothing but the abrasiveness of void. Mainly, though, they humbly proffer something like hope, for us on this planet and, by the opposite of extension, me, which becomes, in this hope, dissolved but not eradicated.

And I found others along the ways and paths, climbs, caves and camps. They gave the small but important kindnesses and greetings of strangers in open spaces where humans are small and far between. Others gave words in wonderful prose about their encounters, their spacious words opening big, airy, breezy or wind-torn vistas, on openness beyond the small of our pain and our limiting hollowness. There is a whole rich literary landscape of writings connecting the therapeutic power of open spaces with that of solitude and with quiet, and it is worth traversing – no maps, compasses or walking boots needed.

It doesn't matter where you go. I have been lucky to have travelled, and to be travelling still. But you don't need to go far. I struck out from my garden looking across railway lines, a housing estate and the gasworks to a beyondness I half imagined. We still live in a land where some openness, some trees and green and space are often just a bus ride or less away, and, if all goes well with our rewilding agenda, future generations may enjoy a far woodier, mulchy and bio-diverse landscape. Who knows, future wanderers may even hear the primeval cry of wolf. And while the myriad colours, the cold frosty autumnal crisp or the fusty summer dust might not be for you, give it a try some time. Walk quietly or sit still in a space that is somehow bigger than you, even more vulnerable, yet enduring and powerful, too. And for a moment, be, and be OK. As the Scottish mountaineer W.H. Murray suggested, 'Find beauty. Be still.'

CYCLING

Sarah Strong

I bought it from my sister. I remember feeling aggrieved that she didn't just give it to me – it was old and, anyway, she had a newer and much more impressive-looking mountain bike.

Cycling seemed a bit too much bother at the time as I'd been signed off with a severe period of depression about three months earlier, but I started commuting to work on my bike. I just followed my nose on the main arteries across the city. I don't drive; I've lived in the city much of my life and never really needed to or could afford to.

The bike gave me the ability to explore beyond the realms of public transport, to discover the lanes deep within the countryside surrounding the city – both on and off road. If I were to identify the most significant element that cycling has brought to my life, it is that: the ability to move beyond the intensity of the city, to slip through the suburbs and to embrace the rise and fall of the countryside.

The exercise improved my sleeping patterns, too. I was sick less often – I put this down to not being in the confined spaces of a busy train or bus. We still have a tendency to talk about mental health and physical health as if they are separate entities. They aren't, of course, and when one is poor, the effects on the other can often be seen quite plainly. My experience is that cycling can attend to both. Sometimes the positive impact can be marked, sometimes less obvious – but it's there.

Without fail, each time I reach the fringes of the city and crest the very outer edge, I inhale deeply and my heart swells in response to the vista that rolls out in front of me. I am out, I am leaving my stresses behind. This is me, now. Me and the bike, wherever I decide to go today.

The reward of cycling is in the simplicity. No thinking. Just doing. I can fall into bed later with the healthy tiredness that comes from physical effort. It keeps my mood buoyed in the autumn and winter months once the clocks have changed. Cycling will never cure mental ill health, but it sure as hell makes for a great management tool.

I also enjoy riding with others, sharing the experience of the journey. The dialogue between you doesn't always have to be audible either. If you're out on the bike with people you ride with regularly, you can pedal for ages and not speak. A look here and there, hand signals to point out potholes or to alert you to traffic might be all that's needed. Other occasions, you might be nattering away quite happily side by side. There's a great deal in that – chatting about more difficult subjects, such as your own wellbeing or lack thereof, might come much more naturally when your primary focus is on some other activity. It isn't clinical therapy, it isn't confrontation, it is not staged. The moving, pedalling body is the machine which forms and expels the words. There's definitely a mindfulness element to riding for me. I am on autopilot. The ebb and flow of the gradients, the road surfaces, the vistas...they are like old friends to me.

Even city riding can elicit similar responses, even though I have to be much more present and aware of the surrounds. On the bike you are hyperaware of the effort you put in – each rise and fall in gradient, the headwind, the weight of the bike, the clothing you wear. You feel the abrupt shift in feedback through the bike as the surface changes. One of the simple pleasures of riding comes with discovering a newly laid section of road; I never had such an appreciation for fresh tarmac before I started cycling regularly!

There's also the matter of speed. You roll quickly on new tarmac. I delight in descents and relish a lovely bit of open downhill countryside where I might push well over 40 miles an hour. Being in control of the bike at that speed is an amazing feeling as the wind buffets your face and makes your eyes water. In the city, however, I take the opposite approach. I encourage myself to 'pootle' and to resist becoming sucked into an unspoken commuting race. Just ride my own ride. When I can do this, I find I am less anxious. I know that I arrive at my destination with a sense of equilibrium – a reward I would miss out on if I had spent the whole journey trying to overtake other cyclists.

The cycling world is a diverse world. It contains something for everyone. Trying to save money on public transport? There's a bike for that. Want to ride across continents? One for that, too. Want to ride with your kids? Yep. Want to get from A to B around town? OK. Need a tricycle, handcycle, recumbent? Want to ride to work but don't fancy getting sweaty? Want to ride with others, or race with them? Want to use your car less or want to cut your carbon footprint? No problem. Can't ride a bike? Many areas have free adult cycle skills sessions. Want to exercise more but don't fancy joining a gym? Ride to work. Save money and get fit.

Cycling won't save your life, but it will make it immeasurably better.

KNITTING

Lynne Cobb

Several years ago, I started knitting again – a skill I had learned as a child. As an adult, I found that it helped me handle stress and anxiety. Self-care is a huge component to getting back to good mental health. Similar to healing from a physical injury or illness, self-care allows you to be kind to yourself as you step along the pathway to healing.

I usually stash a small project into my handbag to keep me occupied when I have to wait somewhere, especially at a doctor's appointment. My stress level was very high when my father was being treated for Alzheimer's disease. Calming myself before appointments, I would breathe, count and stitch, all while feeling a bit more grounded.

Unfortunately, I find myself under tremendous stress again, as I'm healing from the sexual abuse trauma I endured in my childhood at the hands of a distant relative. That abuse – that core wound – groomed me to become a target for additional abuse in my adult life.

Undergoing therapy – which includes memories to be worked through, plus triggers/flashbacks and retraining my thoughts – are all are excruciatingly painful. Seeing my progress – which feels like a slow, uphill climb – keeps me motivated. Taking good care of myself in the process – similar to what I would do if I was recovering from surgery – allows me to be kind and gentle with me.

Self-care reminds me that I am worthy, lovable and strong – even on the days I may not feel like it. When I take a moment to take care of me, in essence I am sending a message to my broken self that I am worthy of love and care. Those are important messages for someone in trauma recovery, because the abuse that led to the trauma feeds its sufferers the opposite messages: that the abused are weak, unworthy and unlovable.

I also find that being creative in several forms of media (writing, painting, photography, sketching, etc.) helps me to ground myself. But knitting, in particular, is my go-to creative endeavor that brings me peace.

At the start of my healing journey, I attended a 'Knitting for Peace' class at a local yarn shop. It was perfect for me, as the class was just freeing. I was part of a small group that met weekly. When I am in a bad emotional place, I rarely want to leave the comfort of my home. But I was motivated to get out weekly and gather to knit.

Our instructor was well versed in teaching self-care and stress management. She walked us through guided meditations, and other ways to calm down and de-stress from the day's events. Just experiencing the complete sense of touch grounded me. The contrast of the warm, soft and soothing yarn and the cooler, stronger feel of the needles was a small yet sufficient distraction from my troubles. The counting of stitches and repetitive motion of knitting helped me find my center. I was breathing deeper and easier. When our small group gathered, we knitted for charitable causes – another way to feel a sense of purpose when you are trying to find your footing in life.

But – by far – the most fascinating thing I learned about the craft – whether it is used as a form of self-care or not – is that the sense of calm I felt was due to the bilateral movement of using two needles while knitting. Not much different from swinging your arms when you walk. No wonder I was feeling calmer. And when I need an additional boost, I pop in my earbuds and listen to bilateral music while I knit.

To mark my healing journey, the instructor suggested creating a mood scarf. It is another way to gauge – pun intended – how far I have come in my healing. Using my favorite colors of blue and pink, I also added two variances of gray – giving me four colors to choose 'emotions' from, based on how I felt for the day. I log the color I will use, and how I was feeling for the majority of the day. Each evening, I knit the color corresponding to how I felt.

My scarf is pretty dark at the start-point. I was working through a tremendous amount of grief and sadness. And, unfortunately, during the worst month of my life, I made an enormous error in the scarf. Not only did I have way too many stitches, I was knitting wrong-sided. How I managed that, I don't know. Well – yes, I do. It was the worst month of my life. Tempted as I was to tear that mess out, I left it – just as my instructor suggested. She reminded me that life isn't perfect, and every great piece of art has a flaw, usually only seen by the artist. So the imperfection is noted as 'The Month from Hell', and the huge mistake stays. It will always remind me that I am strong – I may make mistakes, but I am not defined by them. And I am not defined by my struggles.

It's encouraging that I am now seeing lighter colors in my scarf, meaning I am having better days. When I feel overwhelmed, I look at my scarf and see how far I have progressed. And it makes me smile, even on days I feel I can't.

Knitting and other self-care modules are helping me heal. I am proving to myself that not only will I survive, but I will thrive! And my knitting reinforces that the lies I was told about myself – that I am unlovable and unworthy and weak – are just that: lies. I am lovable and worthy and strong – and I prove that to myself with each breath I take, and each stitch I make.

I am knitting myself back together – literally and figuratively. When I finish my healing journey, I will also finish my mood scarf. My scarf and I will have rough spots and flaws. And that is fine – we will also be strong and enduring and beautiful for what we are.

ART MAKING

Drew Walker

My name is Drew Walker, I am an artist and I have obsessive compulsive disorder and Asperger syndrome.

Without my art process as a vehicle to think through things, I have a feeling that my life would have taken a very different track towards a terrible loneliness and be without purpose. My mum and dad were both art teachers for 35 and 37 years, and, unsurprisingly, I too went to art school. But through the sudden harsh reality of mental illness, I had to leave that part of my life and my art behind.

Finding a personal healing process isn't easy but I was lucky because one actually found me. As I was slowly feeling better on my own journey of recovery, stabilised by three years of different medicines, cognitive behavioural therapy and exposure response prevention therapy, it dawned on me that in a way I was being *saved* every day of the past 1095 days, by walking in the local woods and *accidentally* making things. It turns out that

I was making art out of deadwood and other things I picked up in nature. My healing journey was developing into an ongoing, stretching pathway towards making things, and that was very good for both my own health and that of my family.

Looking back, it was during those first three years of illness, while making imaginary creatures from deadwood in all weathers with Mum and Dad, that I unthinkingly forged an alliance with nature. Through repeated woodland visits and multiple versions of these creatures, the deadwood itself began to resemble the shape and essence of a stag in motion. This stag essence naturally emerged during those intensified times of illness, when I would escape every single day from home – which became my physical and psychological prison – simply by being in the woods. Picking up random pieces of deadwood, I began to symbolise how I was trying to take back control of my life. I was regaining hope, by transforming the deadwood into seemingly living stags. I was thinking about *how* I was healing, and *how* I was trying to recover my life by giving purpose and life to wood that was dead. Eventually, I decided to create a healing garden at the back of my house, inspired by the feelings I had when in the woods.

When I found my new way forward through making art and being with other people, and especially making art together, it unlocked my mind to a new life process that allowed nature to forge a semblance of structure in the face of psychological trauma.

For me, mental illness thrives in void spaces. Without structure in my life, mental illness fills that void to become all that matters through negativity. I was fortunate that mental illness only temporarily halted my life. Art was the connecting thread to some kind of productive future of value for me.

Mental illness can cast a shadow which can blight a lifetime. But It was through a collaborative art process that I found a way to lessen that shadow, lightening it to a faded outline. I was no longer shackled to my every waking thought. I was lucky to be living with art.

Art had become my toolkit and nature's process was regenerating me; I reclaimed my life. I am a gardener of recovery, regained through art.

WRITING

Carolyn

I've had anxiety and depression for as long as I can remember, and yet for a long time I didn't actually know that the horrible range of symptoms that have dominated my life since the age of seven had names, nor that they affected other people.

Like many anxiety and depression sufferers, I thought my periods of extreme fear and/or black mood were just a part of who I was, or a consequence of the situation I was in, or a result of hormones, trauma, or genetics. In truth, my anxiety and depression are probably a combination of all the above. I score an 8 on the Adverse Childhood Experience test. I've experienced a number of traumatic events, and have a particular trigger that can quickly plunge me into a panic attack. It's a challenge to find a neat cause-and-effect trajectory for mental illness, as it is with any illness. Why does cancer affect otherwise healthy individuals? We don't always know. It's the same for mental illness.

At the age of seven – the age at which I started waking up in the middle of the night, unable to breathe (a panic attack, but I didn't know the name of it then) – I started to write. I would make little books. They weren't diaries. They were purely fictional and contained no information about my life. I was forbidden from telling anyone about what was happening in my home, but the fear that I lived with needed an outlet. I simply hated being in my own home, because usually my father was there at the same time, and there was no telling when he might explode and hurt us. I remember counting down the hours each weekend until I could go back to school. At bedtime, I would lie awake, trying to gauge the sound of his voice rising through the thin floorboards, to determine whether he might kill my mother. The enforced silence was almost as bad as the trauma.

The turbulence of my home life, the psychological games I could see my father engaged in with my mother, and the way I could read the change in the air around him right before an explosion all needed an outlet. For me, this outlet was in the form of writing stories.

I wrote seven books between the ages of seven and 14. In hindsight, each provided a 'safe space' for me to process what was going on. I couldn't tell anyone what was happening, and domestic violence was so prevalent where I lived that even if I *did* tell someone, it didn't seem at all likely that they would do anything about my father's abuse. So I wrote. Not descriptions of the horrific scenes I witnessed, but my own fearful experiences couched within fiction. My stories were about ghosts, death, and monsters. That I could identify and name the emotions that were occasionally overwhelming was a gift; the act of writing, too, was and still is meditative, distracting, and empowering. The chaos of strong emotion is somehow ordered and streamlined through writing. I just knew that I loved writing, that I felt better when I did it, and that afterwards my mind felt clearer.

As I got older, I turned to poetry as a form of expression. I loved storytelling, but I also loved language. I fell in love with dictionaries, over and over, because so often they yielded a word or a name for something that I had experienced, defining it. It gave an incredible sense of comfort to know that I wasn't alone in what I'd suffered. I discovered Sylvia Plath, and it was as though a split had appeared in the fabric of reality and allowed me to step through into a whole other world, one that recognized my feelings.

This act of communication – or perhaps communion – that creative writing facilitates between strangers, regardless of class, creed, colour, or even temporality, fills me with awe.

The power of creative writing makes me value it more

than genres of 'writing for mindfulness'. The difference lies in the purpose of the end product. That's not to say I've always written poetry and fiction for someone else to read – I once kept a journal filled with poems that were entirely to be kept hidden, and were just for me to express myself – but to create something that might just connect with another human being and let them feel seen and less alone is an empowering and transform-ative practice. It's what keeps me writing, even when I face the challenges that come with a writing life.

I've published four novels and two poetry collections; my work has won awards, been optioned for TV and film, and has been translated into 23 languages, and yet there are still challenges involved in professional writing. Rejection is very much a part of the writing life.

However, even if I never got published again, I would continue to write. This is precisely because my books are still 'safe spaces'. Like the little stories I was writing as a child, my stories as an adult act as subconscious filters for whatever is going on in my life. I'm still often astonished by the connections between imagination and the subconscious which emerge on the page. I never *purposely* set out to write directly about my life, but often it finds its way on to the page.

There are examples in my work of story lines that, in hindsight, I can see are offering me a way of working through something, making use of the material handed to me by life in order to fashion a narrative that is beyond the messiness of emotion and real-time experience, and which has a neat beginning, middle, and end. In some ways, I think I'm creating my own kind of hope when I do this. I'm reminding myself that this too will pass, that it's just a narrative thread – or a plot twist! – that will take its course without defining me.

My creative work has provided a safe framework for me to work through trauma in my own ways, and in my own time. I'm in control of the narrative. I can allow the traumatic incident to take a different shape or happen to a character. To write about a traumatic event *as it happened* holds no appeal for me, because I can't change the past. But in creative writing, I can do whatever I want. I can mesh trauma and fantasy together in comic, fantastical, or even historical ways. I can bend and twist fact and fiction, and I use my memories in ways that are artful and pleasing to the reader, and me.

When I am mentally ill, I often have no energy. Sometimes anxiety seems to cause too much energy, but certainly not in a good way, and I am distracted and preoccupied by intrusive thoughts and the (horrendous) physical effects of anxiety, such as cold flashes, stomach pains, headache, heart palpitations, diarrhoea, insomnia, and so on. Even low-grade depression and anxiety can bring about a case of 'The Difficult Small Tasks'.

On these days, I may not have a panic attack or feel particularly down, but basic functionality is extremely difficult. I am physically unable to post a letter or send emails. I become incapable of housework. Going out socially is excoriating, and I'll usually cancel. It feels as though everything is very, very wrong, and my body is simply reacting to the state of things – as though there's an invisible barrier between me and the world.

The energy-zapping, Everything-Is-Too-Hard effect of anxiety and depression has and does affect my writing. But perhaps because I have in the past managed to push on and write even when I'm unable to dress myself, and therefore know what writing can do to my energy levels, I am usually able to write even on my darkest of days.

Writing energizes me in a way that nothing else can. A part of my brain tends to feel more alert as I write, the problem-solving, rational side, and I feel enabled and proactive, rather than at the mercy of my mood.

Whereas creative writing *is* a creative endeavour, so much of writing creatively exerts problem-solving, rational areas of the brain. Writing a novel is as much about symmetry and organized change as it is about expression and voice. If you've ever attempted to write (or, indeed, read!) a sonnet, sestina, or villanelle, you'll know that poetry can often involve highly technical skills. I can write – and have written – a poem about a traumatic event, and become so immersed in the language, structure, rhyme, rhythm, and other formal elements required by the *creative* modality of the poem that the memory of trauma is deflected. Instead, I'm engaged in transforming trauma into art, in exploring its meaning, in reshaping and dissecting the relationship between past and present.

Suffice it to say that if I were to write about the same trauma *without* these creative structures, I would find it incredibly draining, and my mood would likely plummet; all my memories of the trauma would be triggered and reignited without outlet or structure.

Conversely, the craft of creative writing is cognitively – and often physically – energizing. I believe this is partly because it exerts technical skills that distract the brain long enough for the other problem-solving regions to become more active. To create something that did not exist before is exciting. Even if the *something that is being created* is never published – and as a professional writer, I write always with this possibility in front of me – it is still exhilarating and energizing to breathe life into a creative piece and regard it as taking its own shape, its own existence as an artefact.

Writing a poem, however short, can be a powerful boost to one's self-esteem, and this positive uplift can make that invisible barrier a little less restrictive, enabling me to do other things. Suddenly, I might be able to post that letter, or send those emails. The buzz of writing a poem might be enough to make that social event possible.

Stories about hardships endured and overcome by other people are usually inspirational and uplifting. When I went through a breakdown, I turned to some books written by individuals who went through extreme difficulties. I found enormous comfort in these, and it brought hope to be reminded that the storm I was caught in would also pass. I didn't for one second consider that my *own* traumatic experience might one day be useful, but once I recovered, parts of that experience beginning to filter into my writing, I felt that there might actually be value in offering these to someone who was struggling.

Drawing upon one's personal experiences to create a piece of art offers another strange and difficult-to-describe element of positivity: discovering that an otherwise painful and somewhat disabling life experience can prove to be *useful*. It's a sudden and unexpected boon, like finding a fifty-quid note in your purse when you supposed it was empty. It's a surprise of the best sort, and where trauma may well have taught you that surprises are invariably nasty, it's particularly pleasant to see how one's own trauma can somehow create meaning, or beauty, or wisdom.

But perhaps the most valuable aspect of creative writing

for trauma is in terms of how it filters darkness. The structures offered by creative writing genres – such as poetic form, or the formal qualities of the short story, which differ quite substantially from the novel, which in turn has its own discrete structural qualities – enable the chaotic matter of trauma to be organized in such a way that one can begin to gain clarity and a sense of control over it. I used to feel ambushed by anxiety, and I became so frustrated about this – literally afraid of the fear itself – that I would force myself to grab a pen and notebook every time a panic attack set in, and even if I was scribbling nonsense, the act of notetaking or mark-making served to filter and purify and gradually untangle the web that anxiety would wrap across my thoughts.

I'm very reluctant to use the word 'cathartic' or even 'therapy' when describing the value of writing for wellbeing. The benefits of creative writing are found in the methodologies of articulation, the solace found in language when one discovers new vocabularies which assist in reorienting oneself in relation to one's illness, and in creating something useful, perhaps beautiful, and much more than the sum of its parts, from the fabric of trauma and mental illness.

The work of writing is ongoing. That is to say that I'm not persuaded that its full benefits can be enjoyed in a single sitting. An ongoing practice is best and I learned a long time ago that writing is rewriting. It must surely activate those parts of the brain involved in transformational thinking which, like any muscle exercised over time, respond more quickly with each practice and support other muscles (of thought).

Sometimes things will appear on the page that astonish me, as though my subconscious can only articulate itself clearly on a white screen. This process is both a cognitive and artistic exploration of recovery and resilience-building, and I would encourage everyone to attempt it.

I am empowered and enlightened by writing.

HORSEMANSHIP

Sally Rigg

I've always known there is a lot within me that wants to be communicated, and yet I found that words never seemed enough to express the processes that were happening inside of my mind. I was unable to communicate how to get my needs met.

Looking back, I believe this was a large contributor towards my mental health decline that started in my teenage years – how I would often become frustrated at myself, anxious and upset. How I felt my ideas were invalidated, not respected, and often dismissed as I was deemed 'too sensitive' or 'not forthright enough'. I internalised these emotions (horribly at times), concluding I was inadequate, that I had only myself to blame. I have only recently realised I have a neurodiverse brain, that I am a highly intuitive woman living in a culture/society tailored towards neurotypicals.

In hindsight, I believe these internalised emotions contributed towards my belief from an early age that animals, particularly horses, could understand me far better than humans would ever be capable of – maybe because I saw a similar awareness within them in that they were full of sensitivities and their own communicational language and understandings. Yet many people would bypass their abilities, write them off as dumb and use them as tools for their own desires instead of finding the ability to learn this language or indeed try to form their own unique level of communication with them. Or maybe it was how I found peace with their non-judgemental stance on life. Whatever the reason, I've often felt more at ease around horses.

Growing up in California meant I learned about the American Frontier, including the intimate bonds indigenous tribesmen would form with their horses that the Settlers met. I had my own Appaloosa/Quarter Horse at the time, so when I came across an inspirational Native American horseman with his relationship-based training techniques, as well as watching the film *The Horse Whisperer* which had come out about the same time, I naturally became more interested in holistic horsemanship methods.

I met my current horse trainer, Jane, through a friend after spending 18 months cycling through various people and never finding a match. Drawing inspiration from western 'Vaquero' horsemanship, classical dressage and natural horsemanship methods with which to form her own techniques, she prefers not having a specific label as she reasons no one can compare and hence judge her via a specific style. I have found with my own relationships that although labels are useful in terms of helping connect with others who identify with certain elements of your personality (or avoid those who don't!), they can also inhibit people who aren't able to look beyond the label and see how one can exist in a spectrum within it. It can become alienating, and I do believe it is quite a human concept to judge and compare yourself with others, one that society is pretty good at enhancing and one that I don't think exists in the horse world.

Jane's yard holds large grassy pastures in which the herd of nine horses are free to roam, and although she does have to supplement their lifestyle (such as providing hay in the winter and trimming hooves), she likes to keep them in as natural a state as possible. I've approached my sessions with her almost totally from scratch, currently learning and refining groundwork techniques in order to apply them to horse agility courses.

I'd like to share my journey with Jane, my current horse trainer, and her herd. Working with each of her horses has influenced my personal therapy.

JUPITER: BUILDING FOUNDATIONS IS IMPORTANT

Jupiter is a chestnut Anglo-Arab. When I approached him, I felt very displaced, finding strong emotions manifesting of not wanting to get in the way of his relationship with Jane and 'steal' her away from him.

I was reminded here that we all must start somewhere, that all relationships take time to develop – that indeed I need to learn the basic groundwork skills to create a foundation upon which to build a relationship and grow it from. I recognised that it wasn't a case of either her or me, that I can have multiple relationships with others as each one is unique and valid.

ODALISCA: BOUNDARIES ARE HEALTHY

When I first met Odalisca, a sturdy ageing Oldenburg liver chestnut, I found she had a strong and steady presence; she beat the rhythm of life to her own drum. She had lived her life and was very content in her twilight years to exist within her own company, which I respected. With a quiet schoolmistress attitude, I felt really secure with her and was able to take first steps of working at liberty, showing me how it felt and what I was aiming for with the others. However, she was constantly taking things just a little too far, and I always found her pushing my personal boundaries and encroaching on my space. She was never aggressive but would take one further step when I stopped or walk faster than me to get slightly ahead.

She really did highlight to me some of my personal issues with boundaries: with many of my relationships, I often say yes, even if it goes very much out of my own way to fulfil the request. If Odalisca did walk into my space, I would instantly take a step back to accommodate her instead of standing my ground. Odalisca really did help me see that I still have more to learn about how to say no, that it doesn't make me a horrible or nasty person for sticking up for myself but shows self-care.

DALLAS: 'GOOD ENOUGH' IS PERFECT

The more assertive female of the group was a dark brown Quarter Horse, Dallas. While I worked with her, she seemed to want to know why I would ask her to do things, and if she deemed there was no reason, then she wouldn't do them. I ended up having quite an emotionally triggering session as I didn't feel I was capable of connecting with her. I kept asking her to move to the side and she didn't seem to understand; I tried different ways (increasing my own pace/energy, trying the other side, altering my cues), but as my confidence dropped, my signals became more confused. She seemed to just stop interacting. We were getting nowhere, and my thoughts instantly spiralled into a paralysing negative-feedback loop of 'I'm not good enough', 'I make things worse', 'It's all my fault'...subdued emotions of being a total failure.

Upon reflection, I really was projecting my own self-hatred on to Dallas and read her reactions to my presence purely based on situations in which I had found myself in the past. When things didn't work, I seemed to decide that it was wholly my own fault and therefore exclusively my responsibility to repair it. When I felt I was forcing Dallas to work with me, it brought back memories of feeling forced to comply with societal regulations that just didn't work for me, and yet here I was hypocritically doing the same to her.

She helped show me that indeed I don't need to pretend to alter myself to fit someone else's expectations. I will consistently make mistakes throughout life, and by saying that because I'm not perfect, I therefore am not worthy of being in relation to others is very unkind to myself. People like me in all my emotional states, for who I am. We all have stories and pasts and can find ways of working with each other despite our differences.

ESCHER: TRUST IN MYSELF AND OTHERS
Escher was the most reserved, thoughtful and emotionally sensitive horse of the group. A dark-bay Quarter Horse, she took no nonsense from anyone and quickly dropped someone who wouldn't respect her quieter ways. Understanding that she had a pickier personality in terms of who she chose to work with really boosted my own confidence when she started walking with me. This encouraged my initial feelings that she wanted to connect and bond with me. I realised this was because she trusted me – she wanted to be here with me.

This links in with my own self-confidence where I constantly question why anyone would want to hang out with me, again harking back to a past where I often felt I didn't fit in. Escher also taught me how each relationship I entered could enhance my experiences with others and teach me how to approach other personality types with compassion. I realised I value all relationships and therefore must not hate all of myself, which is a nice thing to discover!

HOBBITS: RESILIENT AND ROBUST

The Dartmoor Ponies came along in my journey next – four younglings gathered from the moors whom I called Hobbits. I found there was this powerful sense of self-actualisation emanating from them and hence I felt a strong sense of resilience and robustness – they knew who they were and were mentally sound. Nothing was going to alter their being; they wouldn't ever be capable of being 'bullied' or emotionally manipulated by anyone else.

These ponies highlighted to me the notion that I have an innate ability of self-assuredness somehow within me. I was born as a unique entity, but I am somehow much more than this. I loved these horses' 'I can be anything' attitude which I really admire them for.

The world can be cruel, and you find yourself in miserable dark places, but it's not this that defines you, but how we work with the situations we find ourselves in that does. Just like these horses did. Although frustrating at times, working with this little band really brought out this side of me that allowed me to see that I *am* a survivor, I *am* resilient, and I *am* here.

BISCUIT: DON'T EVER STOP ASKING

Biscuit was very light and quite sensitive. I first worked with him on a warm day with a lot of horse-flies, which would constantly land on him, becoming a nuisance. I found that I would ask him to do something (for example, move out and circle around me) and he would look as if he was starting but would stop and paw the ground or twitch his sides trying to remove the flies.

Biscuit showed me how sensitive horses are, that they can feel a fly on the side of their flank or the change in weight of the head collar. They're capable of sensing the world around them, which also ties in with their evolution as a social prey animal. We humans must be pretty loud and obnoxious at times. Working with him also highlighted how I quickly cater to the needs of others by giving instant gratification: when something small happens, I tend to instantly stop, reassess and alter. I have a fear in my personal life that something catastrophic will happen, and I think this issue shows up here, and I also struggle with working through, and sitting with, uncomfortable feelings. I want to work on this, and never stop asking others and questioning the world around me either, as I feel this is a strong element of how I grow and evolve as a person. There are no stupid questions, and if anyone ever stops answering or can't find the answer you need, there are many more who are around to help if we just keep looking.

MY JOURNEY: THE FUTURE

I have found the horse–human bond to be an incredibly therapeutic experience. I struggle trusting people, yet less so with horses, as they are not a threat to my identity, which allows me the safe, non-judgemental space in which to explore who I truly am. Working with these horses has enabled a greater sense of self and sense of my relational struggles, which I am now more capable of approaching in my own therapy sessions in order to improve my own quality of life.

There's an artist whose simple, poignant style strongly resonates with me, who depicts conversations between a Horse and his Boy. One of his pieces shows them looking out over a rugged, open field on a stormy day and the Boy exclaiming, 'Maybe what we are looking for isn't over there at all?' to which the Horse responds, 'It's been here all along, but we have to make the journey.' This has helped me reflect on how my whole life story has gotten me to where I am now, with both my personal health and professional career. How it's not a case of seeking to have the best health or be the best horsewoman but the whole process, including the 'mistakes', and that I have had to make this journey to realise what I am seeking is actually here all along and that I'm doing just fine.

KNITTING

James McIntosh

I used to wake up in the morning with what I called 'the fear'. You know, when you shudder as if a little bit of electric goes down your body?

I always just called it 'the fear'; it was normal for me and nothing I could control. I always accepted this as part of everyday life. I would hear about people with depression, but I honestly thought they just needed a good kick up the bum and to get on with life. That was until the black dog that is depression arrived with me. I did not see the black dog coming; he arrived silently in the middle of the night. I could not get out of bed for a year. I was diagnosed with a 'moderately severe depressive episode'.

What?

Life-loving me?

Fear, anxiety, a catatonic physical state, panic, black. Very black. My head was the deepest black, I had no energy, the depth of sadness in my head was too much to bear. I could not sleep. I could not eat. I could not function. I had lost 'me'.

During that first year of depression, my partner, Thomas, sent his colleague to see me at home and she taught me to knit. That first stitch, and then another, allowed a sense of calm. A creation growing that I had made; I'd found my circadian rhythm with my knitting needles. The resulting product was somewhat shapeless but I remember putting that misshapen article of clothing on my body, looking in the mirror and, for the first time in so long, feeling proud of me again.

Each stitch became a breath, each breath a feeling, each feeling acknowledged and understood.

Slowly, as the knitted items grew from my needles, my confidence grew, too. Each stitch a tangible product that my feelings were worth something. That I was worth something. The tatters of my mind were being knitted back together one stitch at a time. As the stitches grew on my needles, my self-confidence was coming back. I realised that I was worth something. I could see in colour again.

I was able to leave our home again. I was able to have a life. Like the snowdrops in February, I was starting to emerge again, a living, functional creature. I learned to talk about my feelings – to realise that they were valid, they were mine and they needed to be understood.

Each stitch I made became a breath. The next stitch became a feeling and that stitch was a tangible aspect of my feelings, yet an intricate part of the garment I was making. If just one stitch was broken, the whole thing would unravel. So too was the reality that my feelings were part of me. That as the stitch was worth something, so was I.

I was never any good at traditional mindfulness or meditation. You see, I'm a fidgeter. Sitting still and feeling the present did not work for me. I slowly started to learn that the body actually has the answers; it's about spending time with the body. Hand knitting is the same: feeling the yarn and needles as a stitch forms allows thoughts to run through your mind as you are aware of them and feel the bodily sensations of stitch creation and that of your bum on the seat and your feet on the floor. This is a skill I call 'knititation', a mindfulness practice that brought joy back to my life.

Holding two knitting needles in front of me gives me support, it allows a barrier between myself and someone else, a safety net, allowing me to get better. The anxiety stops when I knit. My head is calm.

I am James McIntosh, I am well, I am back and it is because of hand knitting that I am here and I am alive.

A stitch in time saved me.

SOUND AND MUSIC

Thomas Brown

I came across some sadness and anxiety as a child, but I always remember how melancholic music allowed some release and resonance with me. Through my later breakdown, I turned to music for solace and emotional absorption.

Listening to music for me is entwined with coping and staying focused. Also, there is a remaining feeling of the messages in the music. If someone is singing in the second person, it feels as if they are communicating directly with you. Lyrics or prose set to music can, I think, mediate sometimes impossible or illogical thoughts and feelings. I think of lyrics as an awakening of profound parts of the mind.

While in a psychiatric hospital, I would find quiet spots on the ward to let myself go with my headphones on, and dance to the music. I remember saying to a fellow patient that 'I have been moved by music' with a knowingly ambiguous grin. What I meant was that I had been moved emotionally, and also in location – physically.

After hospital I rediscovered composing my own music, but with a slightly intrepid feeling, as if making electronic music was going into an unknown, or that it might even be hazardous to my psyche or mental health. However, I found I could put all my anxiety into the creative process, and achieve something wonderful and satisfying.

I have always loved dance music. One day I discovered how it can make greater sense when you actually dance to it! This began intrepidly when I went to a night club with a lot of anxiety in 2005. An addiction began, to let go of myself on the dance floor – and it was amazingly therapeutic. I sustained the dancing once or sometimes twice every weekend for five years, and the beneficial effects I felt led to this dance experience becoming part of my research and study.

I found while dancing to music that I had the freedom to choose if I wanted to switch off or engage in thinking. I also encountered a wonderful open-spirited culture, meeting some amazing people, and feeling that there is a way forward in a world I never felt I fitted in with, perhaps because of my experiences with schizophrenia. Gradually, all of this helped massively with anxiety and self-confidence, and I started to generally feel on top of things.

I experience great pleasure listening to music still. I find life easier to cope with if I spend a few hours a day relaxing to ambient tracks. I also discovered that listening back to my own music helped me in situations that caused me anxiety, such as in trains and busy places. This felt like more than an added distraction, as if there was a kind of therapeutic feedback loop I had somehow generated.

It is important to know that there are spaces in this world where embracing sound, music or dance can be a powerful outlet for all kinds of mental health issues. I am glad that I found them, I never believed I would; through tracing my own journey, I hope to inspire others to think about their journey being made up of many ups and downs. Through it all, sound and music can still be there with you. And the transition from appreciating music to appreciating all sound can symbolise a sense of freedom for such a journey into the mind.

I seem to have come back into the world through a recovery mediated by music.

QUILTING

Ami

My first episode came out of the blue ten years ago. I was
28 years old when my mood plunged.

Within a couple weeks I'd gone from being a happy
mum, content, with a good job, to depressed, anxious,
paranoid, empty, suicidal and turning to self-harm. My
world turned upside down. I had been motivated, driven,
ambitious, energetic and turned into a polar opposite
of myself.

Two weeks later, and after lots of appointments, I was
considered a high risk to myself and was taken to hospital to be evaluated; it's then I was diagnosed with bipolar
type one. It devastated me, my family and my friends.
I thought that was how my life would be from now on.
It was the worst time of my life. Now, I look back and
realise how far I've come.

After I'd been discharged from hospital, a leaflet came
through the post about sewing courses being held at the

local adult education centre. I went along with my mum for something different to try. It was a six-week course, once a week. I never liked sewing at school and never considered myself a creative person. I'd attempted a few small cross-stitch kits, but that was really my limit. But we learned how to make cushions, bags, doorstops and basic patchwork. And that was it. Suddenly, I'd fallen in love with patchwork and quilting. It had become my therapy. I'd finally found something that was bringing me back. That's how my journey started.

The possibilities are endless with quilting. As the quote says, 'When life throws you scraps, make a quilt.' I look at the quilting process the same way as I looked at battling and overcoming my diagnosis. To a person who hasn't made a quilt before, the task seems massive, confusing, complicated, impossible, and knowing where to start seems daunting. But when you break down the stages, you look at it from a different angle; it's challenging but manageable at the same time. It's a constant step forward with an end goal. It made me realise that my medication was working to an extent, but I also needed to change my mindset, to get back to a place of contentment in my own head.

At first, I didn't realise the impact it was having on me, but after a couple of months I went to see my doctor; filling out a mood chart (which I had to every month), it was there in black and white. My anxiety had massively decreased, my mood was stable, the paranoia and self-harm had completely vanished. Quilting started to block the negative thoughts and replace them with positives. It started to quash my anxiety, calm my thoughts, even when I was unpicking a mistake. It spurred me on to get out of bed in the mornings, rebuilt my confidence, kept me enthusiastic to learn more and even register to do qualifications in patchwork and quilting.

Anxiety had always been my worst symptom; it crippled me to the point where my parents had to pick my son up from school because I couldn't face anyone. It had started to rule my life and I felt I had no control. When I started to get out to quilting groups, things began to change; the world didn't seem as scary and the people didn't judge me. As my social anxiety levels decreased, I was spending more time at quilting groups with like-minded people. They never questioned me about my mental health; it was a relaxed atmosphere with no pressure. It took away the reality of stresses around me and gave me purpose. One positive led to another and I realised I'd managed to get out, whereas before it was hard to leave the house.

For me, quilting has no boundaries; you can follow patterns or create your own. Every quilt looks different. For example, you could make a quilt using the same pattern/design but if you choose different fabric, the quilt will look completely different. Because quilting has so many different stages, it keeps me interested and motivated, and it's a constant learning curve; there's always something new to try. One idea leads to another; my mind is always thinking ahead. The techniques are endless too: from traditional, abstract, modern, geometric, art quilts, hand pieced, machine embroidered, hand dyed, hand embroidered – the list goes on. The only rule really is that it's advisable to use a quarter-inch seam allowance and the rest is your design.

Quilt groups are a great way to meet other quilters and learn new techniques. Quilters love to share their ideas, successes and also techniques that haven't turned out so well to save you time. YouTube is also a great way to gain ideas, and as quilting is becoming more popular, there could well be a course near you.

Quilting is like meditation for me, and the constant learning is my therapy. Instead of having awful anxiety and negativity racing around my mind, it's now full of positivity, ideas to try and what my next project will be. Quilting lifts my mood; it gives me confidence, clarity, passion, excitement and enthusiasm.

Since I started quilting, I've never looked back and I can't imagine my life without it.

PHOTOGRAPHY

Mel

My name is Mel and I am a psychotherapist who works, self-employed, in private practice. I am very much an advocate of pursuing creative pastimes to help improve mental health.

I hope my story inspires you to write, draw, paint, sing or dance your own story and discover the hidden parts of you, when you are ready. Remember that creativity comes in many forms; in my case, it came about through photography.

During difficult times we can all become drained and consumed by our thoughts, worries, grief or anxiety. Googling solutions doesn't really help; I think we are better taking some action to be healthier and more fulfilled through playful endeavours.

It was following a series of traumatic experiences that I had reached the depths of despair. I was emotionally spent and struggling to pick myself up and carry on. I was fed up of my miserable self. I was finding it difficult to get my mojo back. Even emptying the dishwasher felt like a mountain to climb. I had lost interest in doing anything and hadn't seen my friends. My busy brain was robbing me of sleep, and I was tearful a lot of the time.

Rather than follow those signs that I hate so much telling me to 'Keep Calm and Carry On', I decided to practise what I preach and put to use all the learning and knowledge I had gained over the years.

It was time to recognise that I had been through the shittiest experience and I needed some nurturing, and that instead of sitting in this bucket of shame, I could in fact start to nurture and indulge me. I decided I could survive on part-time hours and spend the other half of the week looking after me. It was time to get my mojo back. I'm usually much more of a Tigger than an Eeyore.

I believe once we flex our creative and imaginative muscles, it's a little contagious. I have discovered, through my own history of abuse and from those clients I work with, that it can be hard to be creative and playful when you are in survival mode. I thought it was time to treat myself to a new toy.

I had really wanted a proper camera for a number of years, but the cost had put me off and I didn't know what to buy. My negative inner voice had won for too long: 'you don't need a camera, make do with what you have', 'you will only use it for five minutes – it's just a phase and it will end up in the cupboard', 'they're too complicated'. The biggest stumbling block I faced was not knowing what I was buying and having no one I could ask for advice. I read online reviews but ended up more confused, stuck in analysis paralysis.

One afternoon I plucked up the courage to go to an electrical goods store to seek some advice and perhaps take the plunge and make a purchase. I hesitantly approached the loitering sales assistant and asked what she would recommend for a beginner –something easy to use and one I could grow into. But to my dismay she said she knew nothing about cameras and soon walked off, uninterested.

Flooded by dejection, I left the store empty-handed, returning to my car where I simply sat and fought back tears. I felt useless, unable to simply buy a camera, angry at myself for not being able to decipher what shutter speed, ISO range, resolution and exposure compensation all meant. Needing to talk to someone, I phoned my partner; he listened, sympathised and offered to go with me to get a camera the next weekend. But then he asked if I could go back into the store to purchase something for his computer. Dutifully, I returned and while I sought out the requested item, I mentioned to the guy serving me that this was supposed to be a trip for my new toy, not my partner's. I told him I couldn't find anyone to help me buy a camera. His eyes lit up and he told me he loved photography and said, 'Come with me and I'll help you pick a camera.' Half an hour later, with his help and guidance (and discussion about why he wasn't stationed on the camera section in the first place!), I came home with my beloved – a Nikon DSLR 3400 camera, zoom lens, storage bag, spare battery – and felt like the kid in the sweet shop who had been given the whole jar of pineapple chunks.

I was itching to try out my camera, and although I only knew the auto setting, I started to Google places to go and settled on a farm. My partner and I drove in torrential rain to get there, but it was worth it as I spent a few blissful hours in the hot house photographing the many coloured butterflies. While I am sure more experienced photographers would have veered away from the auto setting, it served me well; the quality of the camera and lens compensated for my lack of technical skill. My butterflies are still my favourites shots and I love them so much they have made their way on to my social media profiles and business cards.

Photography allows me to express my creative side in a visual format, to play about with angles, subjects and light to discover and capture the beauty all around me. I find myself being taken away from my anxious thoughts, my focus and joy of photography preventing negative feelings dominating my mind, the destructive spiralling of overthinking things being replaced with an appreciation of nature.

My camera gives me a reason to make time for a walk to see what I can find to snap; it is my passport to exploring. I photograph just about anything: my dog, the neighbour's flowers, the trees in the park, the narrowboat on the canal, sunsets, sunrises and the moon (though that last one is tricky!).

I love to photograph animals as it combines my creative passion with my love of creatures. In the first year with my camera I totally threw myself into the art; I have been to shoot Amur tigers and polar bears up in the zoo in Scotland, even wolves and foxes. Wildlife parks, nature reserves and safari parks became my playground as I sought out the photos that captured the majestic big cats, the cuteness and awesomeness of nature.

I use the term playground purposely, for I have discovered through my studies and reading the works of authors like Stuart Brown that as humans we are born to create, to make, to play, to share and connect. But many of us can find it difficult to do what children do so effortlessly – to play. I trained with a great psychiatrist, Mooli Lahad, and I will never forget what he told me: 'We can't be on guard and play at the same time.' It is through consuming passions for creativity that we can allow our guard to drop, to be so caught up in the moment that we can put aside our worries and just be.

Photography allows me to create, to make and to play, and it has also allowed me to share and connect. Some weeks after taking up my new hobby, I joined a Facebook group to share my pictures with others and to gain some hints and tips, and this led to an invitation to join a group for a day out. I almost didn't go as I can get socially anxious, but my desire to photograph got the better of me and I lowered my defences to show up. The group meet regularly and I was delighted when I was asked to submit some of my pictures for an amateur exhibition; to share my passion and see people pointing at my photos with a smile on their face brought so much joy to me. Until that show I had never printed any of my photos and I have to say they looked so good I decided to display some on my stairs, and now, as I work from home, many of my clients have also had the opportunity to enjoy viewing them. Too many of us can get so busy trying to earn a living that we do not embrace the things that are so often not deemed productive: art, dance, music, poetry. I believe anything that encourages us to slow down and reconnect to ourselves, our land and others is therapeutic. If you enjoy your pursuit, it is productive and not time wasted at all.

When I ask people how they are creative, they often tell me they aren't. However, you can find creativity in so many places and your skills can develop; if you cook, furnish your home or choose the clothes that you wear, they all require an element of creative skill. I didn't think I had any talent, and while I admit to being no expert on photography, I have managed to create some quite stunning shots with my camera, and I am learning all the time – one day I may even get off the auto setting, but there is no rush.

Encouraged by me, my clients now tell me of how creativity keeps them well. I hear stories of the ice skater who forgets the stress of school and exams as she glides on the ice, the guy who forgets what time it is when he is out birdwatching, and the mum who tells me she feels most calm when she is baking. Everyone can find their creative pastime, whether that be in the traditional arts or through other mediums ranging from carpentry to fishing, and from gardening to improvised comedy.

When we are creating, we are in our 'thinking brain', positive and thoughtful, and our 'survival brain', the high-alert, anxious, guarded mind, goes to sleep for a little while. As we slow down and unwind, we can learn to manage our feelings and our body's responses. If you are seeking a way to rid yourself of anxiety and stress, I recommend taking up a new hobby.

We have five senses and a social engagement system that is soothed by touch, music, smell, taste and things we see. I truly believe when we are creating and engaging in beauty all around us and sharing our gifts with the world, we are in fact restoring our own selves.

So get creative, write, draw, put on some music, go out and splash in the puddles, arrange the perfumed flowers, bake those cakes, dance in the kitchen and take those pictures to find your joy. Play is not just for children and it is not an optional extra; it may just keep us well.

I have learned to play at life and it doesn't matter one jot that I don't get paid. The payment is true joy itself!

PUZZLES

Caitlin

New Year's Eve can be awful.

Don't get me wrong, I love the idea of it – celebrating fresh beginnings, taking time to reflect on the year that was and the one that will come to be, toasting with friends – but the reality of the night typically offers more chaos than clarity.

A couple of years ago, I found myself faced with two choices of how to ring in my New Year: either head out to a bar with a group of people who were bound to drink too much and stay up too late, or stay home alone. Miserable as it sounds, I decided the latter would be more suitable for how I wanted to begin my year. Wavering in the confidence I had in my choice, I was faced with another dilemma: how could I spend the evening in a way where I wouldn't experience any FOMO (fear of missing out) and still enjoy myself?

A few days later, I found my answer at the shopping mall while I was scoping out New Year sales and came across a seasonal store that had a wall full of jigsaw puzzles. A childhood hobby, I hadn't done a puzzle in a good two decades, but it seemed like an easy and affordable way to unplug and clear my mind while feeling productive. I ended up spending the night listening to music and working on my puzzle, a collage of pictures of doors. Best of all? I loved it!

In the years since, puzzles have helped my mental health in a number of different ways. As an introverted, introspective person, I typically have a very vivid inner monologue. Working on a puzzle is just difficult enough that it keeps my mind too busy to start worrying about something, but not so hard that I get frustrated and give up.

I often feel anxious, especially when it comes to social situations. Doing a puzzle with others gives you something to focus on while you spend time together, so you can continue to talk, or not talk, with the ones you love.

I am prone to bouts of depression, particularly when I'm bored or mentally under-stimulated, and unlike reading or watching a movie, puzzles require active participation.

Picking up a puzzle piece may not count as exercise, but that simple mind–body connection fires up a whole new set of neurons. Puzzles can be a powerful tool in keeping your sense of logic sharp as you age. And while it might not seem like much, completing a puzzle or simply finding that piece you've been searching for can offer a tangible sense of accomplishment.

I've gone on to do many puzzles over the years, typically with one on the go during the long winter. As I started outing myself as a puzzler, I got a few different reactions. Some people seemed to think that staying home to work on a puzzle, particularly when the expectation is to go out, is, well, puzzling. But I kept meeting women in their 30s who were also using puzzles as a tool for self-soothing. There's my friend from university who had been using puzzles as a coping mechanism when she was struggling with fertility issues, and my yoga teacher who worked on a puzzle every night before bed to help quell the anxious thoughts running through her mind. A beautiful thing about puzzles is that they can be shared, like my married friends who use puzzles as a way to spend time together.

When I ask myself why I find puzzles to be a helpful tool, a couple of different reasons emerge. First of all, the mental energy it takes to work on a puzzle can help crowd out other thoughts that may be upsetting or negative. As for people who meditate, puzzles can be a way to push aside anxiety.

In my early 20s, my dad was hospitalized with complications due to liver disease. The trauma of witnessing a parent slowly lose his life, coupled with completing my undergraduate degree, wanting to be strong and supportive for my mother, all while trying to enjoy life as a 22-year-old, was a lot to bear. At some point, I picked up a book of Sudoku and would obsessively work on those number puzzles in the waiting room or on the bus ride to the hospital. They kept my mind occupied when there was no solution to the puzzles in my life.

The second reason why puzzles have helped my mental health is by offering an escape. I will admit that I was feeling pretty desperate when I bought myself that puzzle for my solo New Year's Eve. Watching my friends find partners and start families while I remained in the same apartment I've lived in pretty much since my father died, I felt trapped. Choosing to do a puzzle instead of falling back into a lifestyle I didn't want was my first act of change towards making choices that were right for me and the life I wanted to lead. I'm still working on creating a lifestyle that's right for me, but I feel more confident in that journey every day.

Today, a puzzle gives me an analogue alternative to how we spend most of our time – online. Where I live in Toronto, there's a go-go-go work mentality that has infiltrated our leisure time. When you cut unnecessary screen time out of your schedule, you might find yourself with a surplus of hours to fill each week.

I do puzzles simply because I enjoy them and, crucially, I get to soak up their meditative benefits.

AFTERWORD

James Withey and Olivia Sagan

As always in our editing, it has been a privilege to source, gather, edit and present these 33 heartfelt pieces, many written by people who have never written about their lived experiences before now. Together they demonstrate our indomitable drive towards recovery, health and flourishing. Written by people like you, like us, who in most cases have traipsed a well-trodden path to doctors, mental health workers, therapists, medications, support groups, self-help books and websites, these pieces describe the magic and, indeed, mystery of stumbling upon something that works in a small but vital way.

In some cases, that something has saved their life. In all cases, that something reminds us all to keep looking, to keep trying, that there may be something out there for us, something to drag us out of the jaws of the black dog and pop us, even if only momentarily, on safer ground.

There are many, many activities not included in this

anthology but of which we are aware. We deliberately did not include, for example, religious or spiritual activity, but there are many accounts out there of how these could help. We also did not include the overtly esoteric or difficult-to-access, although, again, something there may be just the thing for you. And we did not have the space to include all the wonderful accounts of how being with animals, from cockatoos to crocodiles, has helped people stay sane and smiling, although a piece about woman's best friend as well as contributions on being with horses have been included to remind us of their importance. So, in this final word, we invite you to go and explore for yourself. Sometimes just knowing there might be something out there, something that will become 'what you do to get through', will, in itself, be a help.

If you are reading this during a period of depression, we know you may not have the concentration span or energy, let alone the desire, to read anything. So we hope this book will be friendly to you, opening itself along an easy spine and welcoming you in a spirit of non-judgement and compassion. You will find wide margins in which we hope you will scribble; gaps between paragraphs in which you might pause, smile, roll your eyes, grimace or reflect. We hope you will pick this book up and put it down, start then stop reading it and then return to it in another place on another day – make it dog-eared and well thumbed. Pass it on, when you're done.

Both of us know the tussles of depression and the challenges of a life lived with mental ill health. We hope we have not made light of such darknesses in this upbeat book, showing instead the slithers of hope and even joy that can enter through the everyday; the simple and the doing of something in the here and now.

ADDITIONAL RESOURCES

BOOKS

A Midlife Cyclist: My Two-Wheel Journey to Heal a Broken Mind and Find Joy by Rachel Ann Cullen (Blink Publishing, 2020).

Craftfulness: Mend Yourself by Making Things by Rosemary Davidson (Harper Wave, 2019).

Crochet Saved My Life: The Mental and Physical Health Benefits of Crochet by Kathryn Vercillo and Julie Michelle (CreateSpace Independent Publishing, 2012).

Depression Hates a Moving Target: How Running with My Dog Brought Me Back from the Brink by Nita Sweeney (Mango, 2019).

High and Low: How I Hiked Away from Depression Across Scotland by Keith Foskett (self-published, www. keithfoskett.com, 2019).

I'll Run Till the Sun Goes Down: A Memoir About Depression and Discovering Art by David Sandum (Sandra Jonas Publishing House, 2016).

Jog On: How Running Saved My Life by Bella Mackie (Harper Collins, 2018).

Mindfulness: A Practical Guide to Finding Peace in a Frantic World by Mark Williams and Danny Penman (Piatkus, 2011.)

Outrunning the Demons: Lives Transformed through Running by Phil Hewitt (Bloomsbury Sport, 2019).

Phototherapy and Therapeutic Photography in a Digital Age by Del Loewenthal (Routledge, 2013).

Riding Home: The Power of Horses to Heal by Tim Hayes (St. Martin's Press, 2015).

Running with Mindfulness: Dynamic Running Therapy (DRT) to Improve Low-Mood, Anxiety, Stress, and Depression by William Pullen (Plume Books, 2017).

Taking the Plunge: The Healing Power of Wild Swimming for Mind, Body and Soul by Anna Deacon and Vicky Allan (Black and White Publishing, 2019).

The Mindfulness in Knitting: Meditations on Craft and Calm by Rachael Matthews (Leaping Hare Press, 2016).

The Wild Remedy: How Nature Mends Us – A Diary by Emma Mitchell (Michael O'Mara Books, 2019).

Yoga For Depression: A Compassionate Guide to Relieve Suffering Through Yoga by Amy Weintraub (Broadway Books, 2003).

Yoga for Emotional Balance: Simple Practices to Help Relieve Anxiety and Depression by Bo Forbes (Shambhala Publications, 2011).

WEBSITES

ARTS

Mental Health Foundation, 'How arts can help improve your mental health': www.mentalhealth.org.uk/blog/how-arts-can-help-improve-your-mental-health

Arts Council England, 'Arts, culture and wellbeing': www.artscouncil.org.uk/developing-creativity-and-culture/arts-culture-and-wellbeing

BIRDWATCHING

Westland Horticulture, '6 ways bird watching can boost your mental health': www.gardenhealth.com/advice/birds-and-wildlife/6-ways-bird-watching-can-boost-your-mental-health

Birds in the Hand, 'How bird watching could be incredibly beneficial for your mental health': www.birdseyebirding.com/2019/05/08/how-bird-watching-could-be-incredibly-beneficial-for-your-mental-health

BOXING

The Boxing Planet, '4 ways boxing improves your mind and mental health': www.theboxingplanet.com/4-ways-boxing-improves-your-mind-and-mental-health

CHOIR SINGING

University of Oxford, 'Choir singing improves health, happiness – and is the perfect icebreaker': www.ox.ac.uk/research/choir-singing-improves-health-happiness-%E2%80%93-and-perfect-icebreaker

CLIMBING/HIKING FOR HEALTH

British Mountaineering Council: www.thebmc.co.uk

COOKING

Mental Health Foundation, 'Feeding my mind': www.mentalhealth.org.uk/blog/feeding-my-mind

Beyond Blue, 'Cooking – meditation in disguise': www.
beyondblue.org.au/personal-best/pillar/wellbeing/
cooking-meditation-in-disguise

Anna Freud National Centre for Children and Families,
'Baking and cooking': www.annafreud.org/on-my-mind/
self-care/baking-cooking

CYCLING

Cyclescheme, 'Cycling and mental health benefits': www.
cyclescheme.co.uk/community/featured/cycling-and-the-
mental-health-benefits

National Institute for Health and Care Excellence, 'Commuting by walking or cycling "can boost mental wellbeing"':
www.nice.org.uk/news/article/commuting-by-walking-
or-cycling-can-boost-mental-wellbeing

FILM MAKING

The Creative Independent, 'How to stay sane and healthy
while making a film': https://thecreativeindependent.
com/guides/how-to-stay-sane-and-healthy-while-
making-a-film

GARDENING

Thrive: Using Gardening to Change Lives, 'Why gardening
is good for your mental wellbeing': www.thrive.org.uk/
how-we-help/what-we-do/why-gardening-is-good-for-
our-health/why-gardening-is-good-for-your-mental-
wellbeing

Mind, 'Nature and mental health': www.mind.org.uk/
information-support/tips-for-everyday-living/nature-
and-mental-health/useful-contacts

HORSE RIDING

The British Horse Society, '6 reasons why horse riding is great for your health': www.bhs.org.uk/our-charity/press-centre/news/2019/september/6-reasons-why-horse-riding-is-great-for-your-health

Very Well Mind, 'Using equine therapy as mental health treatment: What horses bring to the therapeutic process': www.verywellmind.com/equine-therapy-mental-health-treatment-4177932

KNITTING

Mental Health America, 'The mental health benefits of knitting': www.mhanational.org/blog/mental-health-benefits-knitting

Knit Om, 'Therapeutic knitting to manage stress, depression and chronic pain': https://knitom.com/therapeutic-knitting

MEDITATION

Headspace, 'The many benefits of meditation': www.headspace.com/meditation/benefits

MINDFULNESS

National Health Service, 'Mindfulness': www.nhs.uk/conditions/stress-anxiety-depression/mindfulness

MUSIC

National Alliance on Mental Illness, 'The impact of music therapy on mental health': www.nami.org/Blogs/NAMI-Blog/December-2016/The-Impact-of-Music-Therapy-on-Mental-Health

Mind, 'Music and my mental health': www.mind.org.uk/
information-support/your-stories/music-and-my-mental-
health

NATURE FOR HEALTH

The Wildlife Trusts, 'Nature for wellbeing': www.
wildlifetrusts.org/nature-health-and-wild-wellbeing

PHOTOGRAPHY

Therapeutic Photography: https://theoneproject.co/
therapeutic-photography

Mental Health UK, 'Let's talk – Using photography to talk
about mental health': https://mentalhealth-uk.org/blog/
lets-talk-using-photography-to-talk-about-mental-health

POETRY

Mind, 'Talking about mental health through spoken word
poetry': www.mind.org.uk/information-support/your-
stories/talking-about-mental-health-through-spoken-
word-poetry

POTTERY

Bridges to Recovery, 'The shape of healing: The power of pottery in mental health treatment': www.bridgestorecovery.
com/blog/the-shape-of-healing-the-power-of-pottery-in-
mental-health-treatment

PTSD UK, 'How pottery can help ease PTSD symptoms': www.
ptsduk.org/how-pottery-can-help-ease-ptsd-symptoms

PUZZLES

Jigsaw Jungle, 'The healing power of jigsaws':
www.jigsawjungle.com/
health-benefits?___store=usd&__from_store=usd

QUILTING

So Sew Easy, 'The many amazing benefits of quilting':
https://so-sew-easy.com/amazing-benefits-of-quilting
Seams and Scissors, '4 health benefits of quilting': www.
seamsandscissors.com/4-health-benefits-of-quilting

RUNNING

Parkrun: www.parkrun.org.uk

SEWING

Sewcialists, 'Who we are: Sewing and mental health': https://
thesewcialists.com/2018/03/12/who-we-are-sewing-with-
and-for-mental-health
Sew Daily, 'Sewing for mental health – how sewing can
improve your mood': www.sewdaily.com/blogs/sewdaily/
sewing-for-mental-health-how-sewing-can-improve-
your-mood

SINGING

Happiful, '5 wellbeing benefits of singing': https://happiful.
com/5-wellbeing-benefits-of-singing

SURFING

The Wave Project: www.waveproject.co.uk/about-us

SWIMMING

Everyone Active, 'The mental health and wellbeing benefits of swimming': www.everyoneactive.com/content-hub/swimming/mental-health-and-well-being-benefits-of-swimming

Mind, 'Cold comfort: How sea swimming boosts my mental health': www.mind.org.uk/information--support/your-stories/cold-comfort-how-sea-swimming-boosts-my-mental-health

WALKING/HIKING

Walking for Health: www.walkingforhealth.org.uk

WRITING

Good Therapy, 'Boosting your mental health with expressive writing': www.goodtherapy.org/blog/boosting-your-mental-health-with-expressive-writing-0823185

Splice, 'How expressive writing can improve your mental health': https://splice-bio.com/expressive-writing-can-improve-your-mental-health

YOGA

Harvard Health Publishing, 'Yoga for anxiety and depression': www.health.harvard.edu/mind-and-mood/yoga-for-anxiety-and-depression

Yoga Matters, Yoga and mental health': www.yogamatters.com/blog/yoga-mental-health

National Institute for Health and Care Excellence, 'Search results: Yoga mental health': www.evidence.nhs.uk/search?q=yoga+mental+health